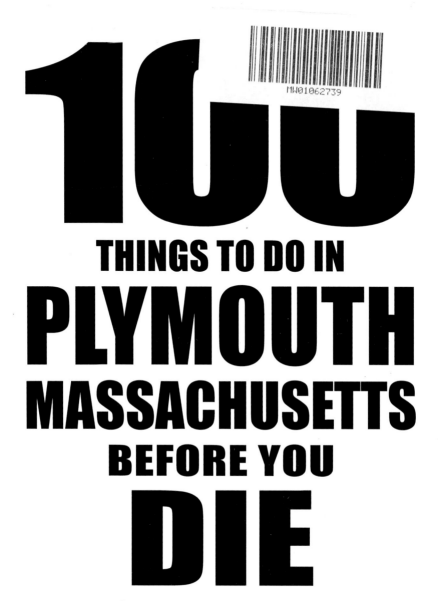

100 THINGS TO DO IN PLYMOUTH MASSACHUSETTS BEFORE YOU DIE

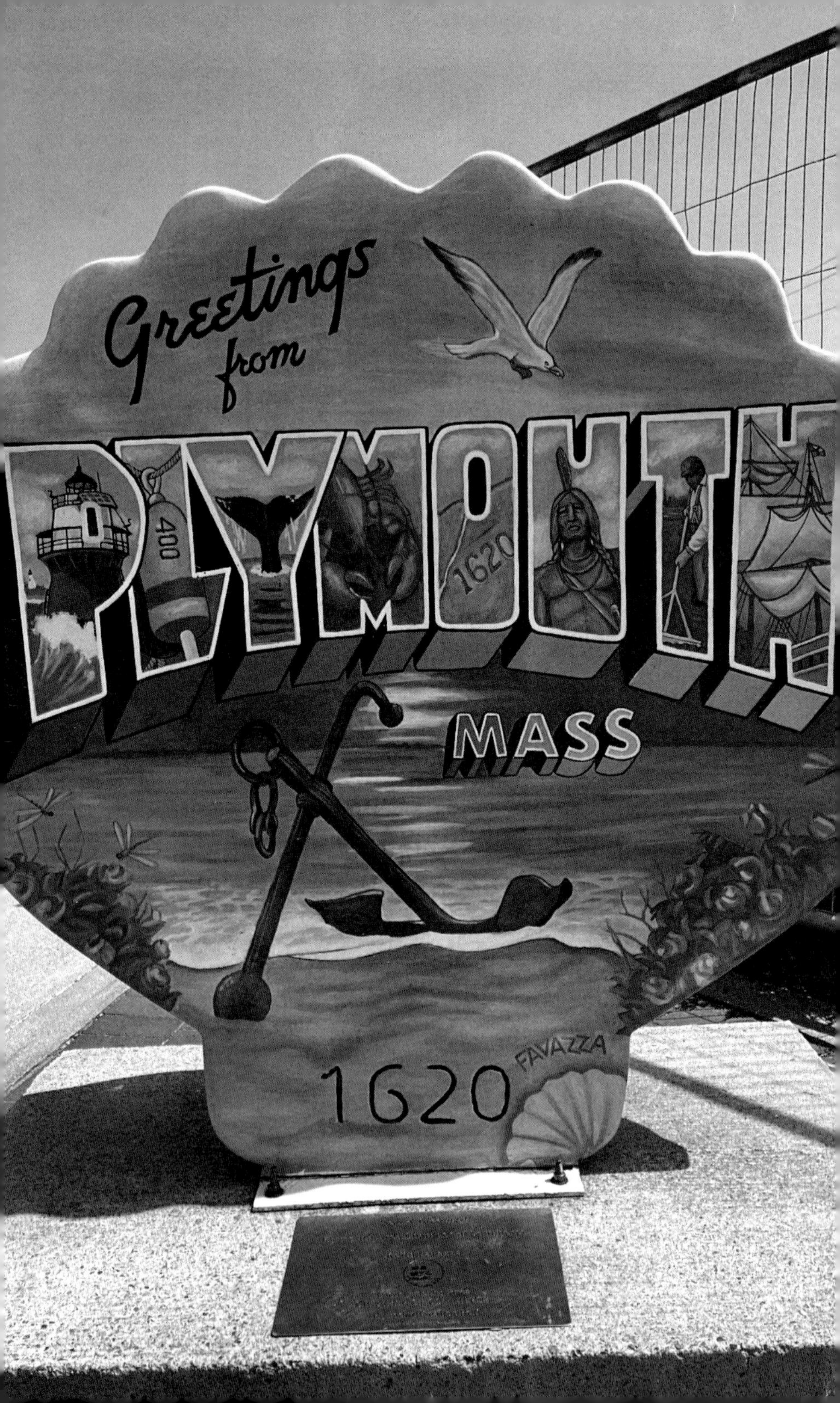
Greetings from
PLYMOUTH
400
1620
MASS
FAVAZZA
1620

100 THINGS TO DO IN PLYMOUTH MASSACHUSETTS BEFORE YOU DIE

STEPHEN PAUL SAYERS

REEDY PRESS

Reedy Press
PO Box 5131
St. Louis, MO 63139, USA
www.reedypress.com

Library of Congress Control Number: 2024930389

ISBN: 9781681065182

Design by Jill Halpin

Cover photograph and all interior photographs provided by Stephen Paul Sayers.

Printed in the United States of America
24 25 26 27 28 5 4 3 2 1

CONTENTS

Sports and Recreation

Culture and History

Shopping and Fashion

WELCOME TO
PLYMOUTH
MASSACHUSETTS
America's Hometown
MOODY & KNOTH, P.C.
ATTORNEYS AT LAW
65
YANKEE
INSURANCE & REAL ESTATE
YANKEE
DOWNTOWN WATERFRONT
DISTRICT
REDISCOVER AMERICA'S HOMETOWN

ACKNOWLEDGMENTS

A sincere thank you to all the shop owners, museum directors, and restaurant folks who answered my questions, both in person and online. Thanks to all the friendly folks on the All Things Plymouth Facebook page who offered their unique perspectives on Plymouth's hidden gems and directed me to places I didn't even know about. I'm glad I get to share your insights with others through this book.

PREFACE

I remember the drive in our lime-green '71 Plymouth Fury station wagon. It was summer, and my two older brothers had banished me to the far backseat. You remember; the one with no seatbelt facing the open rear window. The 18-foot Fury also hauled my two parents, two sisters, a cooler, a dog, a beach blanket, and an umbrella—also lime green—it was the '70s after all! We were heading to Plymouth, and my father had spent the whole trip telling us about all we would see there: an old wooden ship with huge sails, a big rock, and a spooky old cemetery on a hill. Oh, and that chubby little kid in the photo standing beside his sister is me. That was my first day in Plymouth, and it was the day lifelong memories were formed and roots took hold.

Plymouth has always had a special place in my heart. During college, I spent my summer weekends on Plymouth's White Horse Beach. When I worked in Boston, I spent weekends with colleagues at their Plymouth cottages. I bought my first-ever house in 2003—not in Boston where I was working, nor Missouri where I had just accepted a job—but on Manomet Beach in Plymouth. It's where I spend my summers, and it's the place I will retire. Today, when I walk past that old wooden ship or the big rock—which was never that big to begin with—or stroll through that spooky old cemetery on the hill, the memories of that summer day in the '70s come rushing back. I think about the memories my kids have made in these same places over the past 20 years and marvel at the roots that have taken hold.

I wrote *100 Things to Do in Plymouth Massachusetts Before You Die* to share the amazing things I've learned about Plymouth over the years. This account is not necessarily a "best of" list, but a list of what makes Plymouth a unique, one-of-a-kind place. So, enjoy the rich history and great places to eat, drink, and shop. Take in the beautiful beaches, state parks, and conservation areas. Get to know the town's thriving art community and sample its broad entertainment opportunities. But be careful making memories. It's not long before the roots begin to take hold.

Stephen Paul Sayers

DRINK
Coca-Cola
IN BOTTLES
PARADE
MASS.

FOOD AND DRINK

1

ADD A LITTLE SPICE
AT SALT RAW BAR + FINE CUISINE

There's seafood . . . and then there's seafood—and you won't find any better than what Salt Raw Bar + Fine Cuisine serves. Located in the Village Landing Marketplace on Plymouth's waterfront, Salt creates some of the finest Asian-style seafood anywhere. Owner and Head Chef, Johnny Sheehan, has turned Plymouth seafood on its ear—or its gills—with creative dishes and show-stopping flavors. He sources the freshest seafood and local produce and adds his signature touch. Raw curious? Don't miss the kampachi, salmon, or yellowtail sashimi. Or start with the crunchy-raw Tuna Tartare Tostado. Raw hesitant? Try the Wagyu beef blowtorched to a perfect medium rare, or choose from the rice, noodles, dumplings, or soup dishes. Sheehan also claims the best smash burger and fries on the South Shore. Salt has two beautifully appointed dining rooms, a comfortable bar, and the best service around for the ultimate dining experience.

170 Water St., 774-283-4660
saltrawbarplymouth.com

2

EMBRACE THE GARDEN
AT RYE TAVERN

Talk about "farm-to-table" restaurants . . . at Rye Tavern, the table is literally at the farm! The ever-changing menu at Rye matches the seasonal fruits and vegetables harvested just 50 feet from the Rye Garden kitchen for their unique dishes. The Tavern is housed in an 18th-century tavern and inn that served many a traveler from Cape Cod to Boston, including President John Adams. Called "One of the Great Farm-to-Table Restaurants in the US" by Delish.com, the Rye sources their meats and produce from local growers and farmers markets. They have established relationships with local farms such as Skinny Dip Farms, Queen Bee Honey, Duxbury Sea Salt, and other local favorites. Located along a dirt road that hasn't changed much in 300 years, Rye Tavern is a must-visit for fresh food enthusiasts seeking a traditional old-tavern eating experience. And like every good New England restaurant, they serve a wicked-good lobster roll!

517 Old Sandwich Rd., 508-591-7515
theryetavern.com

3

GET YOUR WINE ON

AT UVA WINE BAR

Uva Wine Bar owners Katy Thayer and Michelle Manware might have ushered in the future of wining in downtown Plymouth. The only self-pour wine bar on the South Shore, Uva sells two-, four-, and six-ounce servings from their self-serve wine station, allowing parties to choose multiple favorites without purchasing multiple bottles. Plymouth resident, Margie Hobbs, summed up Uva's unique approach this way: "I have traveled the world and have never come across anything remotely like it." Uva means grape in Spanish, and Uva Wine Bar has at least 48 types of liquid grapes in rotation at any time. The menu is perfect, with build-your-own charcuterie boards, flatbread pizzas, chips and dip, and desserts. Uva also schedules events of local interest, such as cookie decorating, spiritual medium readings, shell art, needle felting, ornament and holiday bracelet making, murder mystery nights, wine tastings, and even live music on the weekends. They also carry local craft beers for "non-uva" drinkers.

46 Main St., 774-283-4211
uvawineplymouth.com

TIP

Uva can be booked for private events on Saturday and Sunday afternoons. Just find 25–60 of your best friends. The Wine Bar has been featured on CBS News Boston's *It Happens Here*, as well as in feature articles in *South Coast Almanac*, *The Patriot Ledger*, *Backyard Road Trips*, and *Life on the Bay* magazine.

4

WHET YOUR APPETITE
AT MALLEBAR BRASSERIE

You gotta pay attention to a restaurant owner who has cooked for the great Julia Child. Jim Casey opened Mallebar in 2018 to provide Plymouth the ultimate French dining experience. Wife and co-owner, Heather Casey, told *Wicked Local*, "The French lifestyle forces people to slow down," and that's what you'll want to do at Mallebar. Enjoy their oysters and escargot to start off, or maybe octopus if you're feeling adventurous. You can't go wrong with the cheese and charcuterie boards before your entrée, either. For the main course, relish the beef and bird dishes with their rich, buttery, cheesy toppings and bordelaise sauces. The gorgeous dining room reflects the Caseys' attention to detail, with spacious, comfortable booths, a classy 12-seat bar, and ample space to move around. For casual dining, visit the Caseys' other restaurant, the Blue-Eyed Crab Caribbean Grille & Rum Bar at Village Landing Marketplace.

15 Main St. Ext., 508-747-0471
mallebarbrasserie.com

5

GO GREEK
AT ANNA'S HARBORSIDE GRILLE

Itching to try authentic Greek cuisine made from scratch? Anna's Harborside Grille can scratch that itch. Co-owners—and brothers—Demetri and George Stavropoulos grew up in the restaurant business and created Anna's as a heartfelt tribute to their late mother, whose amazing Greek recipes they now share with their loyal customers. The menu pops with a slew of authentic Greek specialties like souvlaki and gyros, calamari and moussaka, and their olive oils and spices are imported from family farms in Greece. The brothers still offer traditional American fare like burgers, pizzas, salads, and seafood for the less adventurous, as well as sandwiches and paninis, and an assortment of unconventional—but intriguing—appetizers. Grilled octopus, anyone? Don't miss their customer favorites: lamb kabobs, Aegean fries, lemon and herb grilled chicken, and weekday buck-a-shuck oysters. You'll love the waterfront location, live music on the patio, and tailgate tents during football season.

145 Water St., 508-591-7372
annasharborsidegrille.com

6

FOLLOW YOUR COMPASS

TO 42 DEGREES NORTH

The most "corporate" restaurant on the list—and that's not a dirty word—42 Degrees North is one of the few Plymouth destination restaurants outside the downtown area. Owners Kevin Hynes and son, Erik, of the Hynes Restaurant Group, have been in the business for over 40 years and have perfected a formula for successful South Shore restaurants, and 42 Degrees North is no exception. Since 2012, 42 Degrees North has been a seafood lovers paradise and is known for the large portions, reasonable prices, and classy setting. The Fish Market Menu varies depending on the daily catch, and with their signature baked stuffed lobster and expertly pan-seared, broiled, fried, and chargrilled choices, you can't make a mistake. But 42 Degrees North isn't just seafood. The menu includes succulent beef tips, prime rib, chicken pasta, mac & cheese, and an assortment of appetizers, soups, and salads. Corporate never tasted so good.

690 State Rd., Manomet, 508-224-1500
42degreesnorthrestaurant.com

TIP

42 Degrees North is named after the parallel that runs directly through Manomet. It's actually 41.9186 degrees, but they decided to round up! Try 42 Degrees North's sister restaurant, 71 Degrees West Atlantic Steakhouse, that opened in August 2023 on the Plymouth Waterfront.

7

G-GRAB A B-BURGER
AT KKATIE'S BURGER BAR

Okay, so maybe you can't pronounce the name—it's Kuh-Katies, by the way—but once you've eaten their burgers, you'll shout it from the rooftops! Inspired by the 1918 song "K-K-K-Katy," a stuttering wartime jingle by Billy Murry, KKaties will fill you with enough red meat and cheese to worry your cardiologist. Voted Best Burger on the South Shore, and it's easy to understand why. They press their half-pound, 100 percent Angus beef fresh each day and serve it in unexpected configurations. You haven't lived until you've tasted a horseradish burger with fresh peppercorn pressed into a patty and garnished with caramelized onions, bacon, and cheese or the Hawaiian, with grilled pineapple, bacon, and teriyaki sauce. But the crème de la crème is the one-pound burger known as The Rock, four quarter-pound stacked patties loaded with cheese, bacon, and—why not?—onion rings. KKatie's is steadily becoming one of the most popular eateries in Plymouth!

38 Main St. Ext., 774-773-9444
kkaties.com

TIP

Owner Kate McSorley opened KKaties in Plymouth in 2010 and she has expanded to four additional locations: Hyannis, Marshfield, Plympton, and West Bridgewater. Today, New England. Tomorrow, the world?

8

CHOOSE "CHOWDAH"
AT CABBYSHACK RESTAURANT & PUB

If you're looking for the best New England clam chowder anywhere, head over to the CabbyShack. They produce roughly 500 gallons each week, made fresh daily and served in a fluffy bread bowl. This signature dish has been featured on the Food Network's *Best Thing I Ever Ate–Guilty Pleasures* and *Diners, Drive-Ins, and Dives*. The Shack's menu is extensive, with a variety of family favorites to satisfy everyone in your party—seafood, lobster, pasta, burgers, short ribs, steak, and a surprisingly good bar pizza—but don't expect a static menu. Owner Cabby Brini and his chefs change it up to create new and interesting choices. Your kids will love the fun photo stand-in out front, cool undersea murals inside, and beachy trinkets they can grab on the way out. Open since 2003, CabbyShack has become a downtown staple, serving over 10,000 customers per week.

30 Town Wharf, 508-746-5354
cabbyshack.com

TIP

Don't tell the kids, but you can also sneak out later for the live music, DJs and dancing, and entertainment seven days a week out on the outdoor deck. And don't leave without some sweet merch: hats, hoodies, tie-dyed tees, tank tops, and much more. You can also buy online from their new virtual store.

9

GO RAW
AT KOGI BAR & GRILL

Is seafood all there is to eat in this town? Not by a long shot. Since 2015, Kogi owners Patricia Cho and Thuyet Phan—also head chef—have won over the hearts and stomachs of Plymouth with their amazing Korean food. They are a customer-oriented business, and they remember you—your order, your shellfish allergies, your cooking preferences. As for the food, they have the best sushi in town, hands down! Try the Alaskan, a seaweed roll with a thick portion of salmon, rice, and a chunk of avocado. Or add a dollop of cream cheese and you've got their Philly roll. And whatever you order, add the Kogi fries—think potatoes, but with queso, beef, scallions, onions, hot sauce, and a fried egg on top. And with an extensive beverage menu, you can't help but find the right beer to pair with your meal. Try Kogi once, and you'll be hooked.

8 Court St., 508-927-4105
order.toasttab.com/online/kogi-bar-and-grill#!

10

START YOUR DAY
AT THE BLUEBERRY MUFFIN

When you hear the words "family restaurant," you can't help but put The Blueberry Muffin right at the top. Owners Kevin and Rosemarie Brown have welcomed their three grown children into the business; and with two of them trained chefs, they've taken the Muffin to new heights. The Browns opened the original Blueberry Muffin in Cedarville in 1998 across the street from a Dunkin' Donuts. Despite the competition, the Plymouth faithful lined the sidewalk for the Muffin's amazing breakfast, lunch, and variety of sinful donuts, pastries, and, of course, muffins. Success breeds success, and they opened two additional successful locations in Kingston and South Plymouth. They're known for their hand-shredded corned-beef hash as well as their plate-size pancakes. Their homemade soups are rich and hearty and the muffins…well, it's not called The Blueberry Muffin for nothing! Join them for the ultimate in homemade everything.

2240 State Rd., 508-888-9444
12 Village Green S, 508-927-4566
164 Summer St., Kingston, 781-936-8848
bluebmuffin.com

GIVE UP THE GRAPE
AT PLYMOUTH BAY WINERY

For Michael Carr, owning a winery was a lifelong dream—and it shows. Located on the waterfront with breathtaking harbor views, Plymouth Bay Winery offers numerous fruity alternatives to the grape. Enjoy cranberry, blueberry, peach, apricot, strawberry, and plum wines, just to name a few—all using locally grown, native berries. Don't worry, purists, you can always find the traditional reds and whites you're accustomed to. The Winery is fun and festive, with numerous events to keep you coming back, like paint night with your besties or live music. But wine tastings are their staple, and hour-long sessions are held every afternoon during the summer months. You can even drop in without a reservation. It's great for couples and groups, and don't forget the cheese and cracker plates, chocolates, jams, and sauces! Make sure to check out their website for cool sangria recipes using their signature wines.

114 Water St., 508-746-2100
plymouthbaywinery.com

TIP

When you leave, don't forget to take a little bit of Plymouth Bay Winery with you. They have a huge selection of "to go" wines, chocolates, wine jellies and marinades, olive oils, and honey. If you can't decide, just grab a gift basket with selections already chosen for you!

12

GET IT FRESH
AT WOOD'S SEAFOOD

On the hunt for fresh-caught seafood? You've found it at Wood's Seafood, a no-frills, cafeteria-style dining experience. Enjoy the stunning views of Plymouth Harbor and *Mayflower II* from just about every table—plus, outdoor deck seating. Don't miss their signature Clambake for One with lobster, steamers, clam chowder, and fries, as well as New England seafood staples like fried clams, fish-and-chips, shrimp, and lobster rolls. Arrive mid-afternoon and you'll see fishermen delivering the catch of the day. Wood's is also a fish market—the oldest in Plymouth. They will whip up a Clambake to Go or even cater for up to 90 people at your home. Wood's was voted the Reader's Choice Award for Best Seafood Restaurant (2015–2020) and Best Fish Market (2013–2020) in *Yankee* magazine's *Travel Guide to New England*. If you are from out of town and you fall in love with Wood's on your Plymouth visit, don't panic. They ship live lobsters, clambakes, and other delicacies anywhere in the United States.

15 Town Pier, 508-746-0261
woodsseafood.com

CRACK A CLAW
AT THE LOBSTER HUT

So, what's the best counter-style, cafeteria dining in Plymouth: Lobster Hut or Wood's Seafood? They both provide harbor views and a great selection of fresh-off-the-boat broiled, fried, and baked seafood. In the end, it's like choosing your favorite child; you just can't—they're both amazing. Lobster Hut has served Plymouth and the world for over 50 years, and their wall of plaques attests to their success. For lobster fans, you're in the right place, and the legendary clam chowder will fill you up. The lemon-pepper sole, broiled haddock, and fish-and-chips are melt-in-your-mouth fresh. And if that isn't enough, the Hut has added milkshakes to the menu! Get there early to beat the lines and ensure an outdoor waterfront table under the canopy. Lobster Hut tends to get a little busy—and messy—during the summer season, so bring a few sanitizing wipes for the tables.

25 Town Wharf, 508-746-2270
lobsterhutplymouth.com

14

SIT BACK AND RELAX
AT LEENA'S KITCHEN

Okay, so the location doesn't really have the wow factor that waterfront and downtown restaurants have. But Leena's Kitchen is one of the best Italian restaurants in Plymouth and shouldn't be overlooked. Brother and sister owners, Daniel Casinelli and Lisa Marsh, follow in the steps of their grandmother, Leena, creating a comfortable place to sit back, relax, and enjoy a meal like they did growing up. This is Italian comfort food, with amazing focaccia bread, hand-rolled gnocchi, house-made pastas, seafood, and legendary pizza—like chicken bacon ranch; Bolognese; and kale soup pizza (with beans, linguica, and potato). They even have vegan cheese and vegan veggie pizza. Enjoy it all with an Italian wine chosen from an extensive list. Leena's Sunday brunch is a must for the Benedicts and frittatas, the sinful rotating donut choices, and the relaxing live acoustic music from local musicians.

63 Long Pond Rd., 774-404-7470
leenaskitchenplymouth.com

15

SAVOR THE SWEETS
AT PLIMOTH CANDY COMPANY

A favorite stop for families for over 30 years, Plimoth Candy Company is narrow and cramped, but every inch is filled with something delicious or fun. The chocolate case is packed with sumptuous clusters, chocolate-covered pretzels, English toffee, barks, turtles, truffles, nonpariels, peanut butter cups, and creams, and their mouth-watering fudge never fails to satisfy. But everyone's favorite is the penny-candy wall—full disclosure: the candy costs more than a penny! Kids line up to fill a bucket with their favorite gummies, sours, taffies, bullseyes, caramels, chocolates, and sugary treats. Usually, it's orderly and no one gets hurt. But the store is more than just candy. You'll find maple syrup, jams and jellies, popcorn and cotton candy, shirts, hats, socks, mugs, stuffed animals, wind chimes, souvenirs, and post cards. And check out their vintage vinyl 45s collection! You can even try before you buy on their old-school record player.

84 Water St., 508-747-1107
plimothcandy.com

16

JOIN THE FAMILY
AT MONTE CHRISTOS

Owner Christos Mallios boarded a boat from Greece to New York in 1955 with $20 in his pocket and established three successful Plymouth businesses before opening Monte Christos in 1983. The family have been doing pizza right for 40 years—and at affordable prices. But it ain't just pizza. Sure, they won the South Shore Pizza Palooza Best Pizza award in 2019, and their Big Mac pizza is to die for. But if you want a variety of pastas and strombolis, they have those, too. And don't miss their subs and burgers, seafood, steak tips and kabobs, club sandwiches, teriyakis and stir-fries, mouth-watering appetizers, and specialty adult beverages. Located in Manomet, Monte Christos is a true family restaurant, and you're treated like family during each visit. They don't deliver, but why would you want to take it anywhere else? Check their schedule for Karaoke and Paint Nights.

745 State Rd., 508-224-7000
montechristosrestaurant.com

TIP

Make sure to grab some of their sweet "224" merch: hoodies, shirts, and tees. Check their Facebook page for updates on merch sightings across the globe.

facebook.com/montechristos224

OTHER GREAT PLYMOUTH PIZZA PLACES

Stevie's Pizza Plymouth
46 Main St., 508-830-0555
steviespizzaplymouth.com

Rose and Vicki's
747 State Rd., 508-224-3502
2230 State Rd., 508-888-2822
358 Court St., 508-746-6066
roseandvicki.com

Cappy's House of Pizza
741 State Rd., 508-224-6868
cappyshouseofpizza.com

Plymouth House of Pizza
50 Long Pond Rd., 508-746-0444
facebook.com/people/plymouth-house-of-pizza-pizzeria-and-pub/100063676027932

Family Pizza Plymouth
4 Pilgrim Hill Rd., 508-747-7474
familypizzaplymouth.com

The Artisan Pig
66 Court St., 774-404-7012
artisanpig.com

TRY THE PIE
AT DILLON'S LOCAL

A huge local favorite since opening in 2015, Dillon's Local is Plymouth's downtown neighborhood pub. An Irish Pub at heart, Dillon's serves classic comfort food like their famous Reuben and Guiness beer-battered fish-and-chips. For shepherd's pie fans out there, owners Colin Dillon and wife, Samantha, serve it up as an appetizer, entrée, and even as a pizza. Dillon's celebrates St. Paddy's Day like no other, rolling out an incredible lineup of Irish drinks—and even featuring songs by the immortal Irish crooner, Norman Payne. And don't miss the Irish breakfasts on Sunday. Other mouth-watering choices are the chicken picatta, French onion soup, fish tacos, and ahi tuna once the summer menu arrives. Dillon's will also cater your birthday, graduation, wedding, or anything else you want to celebrate. They're "closed for freedom" on July 3rd and 4th to give their hardworking staff some well-deserved time off.

21 S Park Ave., 774-404-7913
dillonslocalplymouth.com

REDISCOVER SANDY'S RESTAURANT

ON PLYMOUTH LONG BEACH

Who remembers their first beach burger—the slightly gritty taste from the sand sticking to the ketchup or the seagulls trying to steal a bite? For many, Sandy's Restaurant on Long Beach is that memory. Sandy's has fed Plymouth beachgoers for over 30 years, and in 2023, new owners Shawn Gallagher and Tara Frare stepped up to continue that mission. They've spruced the place up a bit and added a variety of salads, as well as salmon, swordfish, lobster, steak tips, and shrimp to the menu's burgers, fries, and seafood staples. They've also upgraded to table delivery, so no more waiting for your number to be called. A full dinner menu is available after 4 p.m. to broaden Sandy's appeal as more of a dining destination. With beautifully repainted murals on the building's exterior and live acoustic music provided Thursday and Sunday afternoons, they're well on their way.

132 Warren Ave., 1 Ryder Way, 508-747-5911

TIP

Hours are 11 a.m. to 8 p.m. from June until October. Don't bother with your credit card, Sandy's only takes cash—but there's an ATM on-site.

TASTE THE HISTORY
AT GELLAR'S SNACK BAR

For 97 years, Gellar's Snack Bar has been a Plymouth staple, serving up their legendary ice cream to the good people of Manomet. Gellar's also has that retro look and vibe—but it's authentic. The lighted rooftop ice cream cone only adds to the throw-back atmosphere. No water views, no cutesy harbor storefronts, just a side-of-the-road shack where ice cream and comfort food await on a hot day. You can't go wrong with their burgers, hot dogs, and grilled cheese, and the clam, shrimp, and scallop rolls are worth the drive. They have peanut butter and jelly for the kids, and don't miss their sinful from-scratch dessert and donut lineup. When it's warm, join them for movie nights on the outdoor screen. When it's cold, enjoy your food in the heated igloo. Look for the patriotic "God Bless Our Troops" sign and the signature red, white, and blue bunting flags that adorn the exterior.

506 State Rd., 508-224-2772
facebook.com/gellarssnackbar

20

HOIST A CAN
AT MAYFLOWER BREWING COMPANY

Did the Pilgrims really land in Plymouth because they were out of beer? William Bradford's historic quote may suggest so (see Tip). But if not, a place like Mayflower Brewing Company in 1620s Plymouth would have had a good reason to. Mayflower's craft beer is epic, with signature year-round IPAs, porters, and ales as well as small batch seasonal favorites. Everything is craft-brewed and canned at the Brewery, and you can always sample their stock in the tasting room, buy your favorites at the retail store, fill your growler in the taproom, or even take a tour. Their event calendar is always full, with weekly cornhole leagues and tournaments, live music, weekend Beer Gardens with food trucks, and creative endeavors like paint nights. They even hosted a horror convention in 2023! You can BYO vinyl to be played in the taproom on Thursdays, and taproom events are always dog-friendly.

12 Resnik Rd., 508-746-2674
mayflowerbrewing.com

TIP

William Bradford's famous quote on reasons for landing in Plymouth is featured on Mayflower Brewing Company T-shirts: "We could not take time for further search or consideration, our victuals being much spent, especially our beer." Mayflower Brewing Company beer can be found in all six New England States and New York City.

21

GET ZIGGY WITH IT
AT ZIGGY'S ICE CREAM

If you're looking for the best ice cream in downtown Plymouth, Ziggy's is the place to be. They've been a waterfront must-visit since 1957, and you can choose from all sorts of frozen goodness—ice cream, soft serve, frozen yogurt, sherbets, sorbets, and even pup cups for your furry friends. The ice cream cones are huge, with choices of sugar, cake, waffle, cookie, and even chocolate pretzel cones. As for flavors and toppings, whatever you can imagine, they have. And don't forget their amazing, gooey sundaes like fried Oreo! Ziggy's also has a surprisingly wide selection of food, including burgers—even salmon and vegan burgers—lobster rolls, grilled cheese, chicken fingers, nachos, tater tots, onion rings, clam chowder, and pizza. The atmosphere is always buzzing, and the hardworking staff members serve you with a smile. Come to the waterfront to visit this one-stop fill-up for all things yummy.

120 Water St., 508-746-5411
plymouthicecream.com

GIVE THESE DELICIOUS PLYMOUTH ICE CREAM SHOPS A TRY

Seaside Ice Cream & Waffles
358 Court St., 508-830-6807
seasideicecream.com

Kilwin's Chocolate Fudge & Ice Cream
150 Water St., 508-927-4670
kilwins.com/stores/kilwins-plymouth-ma-plymouth-rock

B's Homemade Ice Cream
170 Water St.
bhomemade.com

Kush Kone Ice Cream
733 State Rd., 508-224-5960
facebook.com/kush.kone

Cold Stone Creamery
158 Colony Pl., 508-746-7737
coldstonecreamery.com

Yogi's Café
80 Water St., 508-410-1013
yogiescafemenu.com

Cupcake Charlie's
6 Town Wharf, 508-747-9225
cupcakecharlies.com

Tales of the Sea Emporium
10 Town Wharf, 508-747-0822
facebook.com/talesoftheseaemporium

GRAB A BITE
AT WILL & CO. CAFE

Jason Bissett and wife, Brooke, opened Will & Co. Cafe in 2017 with inventive breakfast and lunch creations that will keep you coming back. Who doesn't love fry babies—think donuts crossed with fried dough—or fried avocado Benedict? For the health- and sustainability-conscious, you can find quinoa, vegan- and gluten-free options, locally sourced ingredients, and even protein pancakes. This is a true family business, with Head Chef Jason working side-by-side with his father, Tom, at the grill and Brooke's mother designing the company shirts. And you can thank java-guru, Brooke, for the choice of world-class organic coffees. The family's sense of humor shines with head-scratching menu items like Grampa's Red Flannel Hash, Scurvy Fighter, Chickens on Strike, and Million Dollar Bacon. Love the free coffee for veterans as well as for nurses and educators during Teacher Appreciation Week! Take advantage of the flavored Red Bull for a mid-morning pick-me-up!

6 Court St., 774-773-9732
willandcocafe.com

STOP
AT STOWELL'S CAFE & DELI

When Dan Stowell bought Big Al's Deli in 2014, he didn't want to rock the boat and alter the menu. But over the past 10 years, he's made Stowell's Cafe into much more than just a deli, and it's a fan favorite in Manomet. The menu is deep, with family favorites like burgers, hot dogs, mac & cheese, soups, and salads. You'll also find panini sandwiches, quesadillas, just about anything parmesan, and every form of haddock imaginable—baked, stuffed, blackened, New Brunswick'd, picatta'd, Valencia'd, and au gratin'd. Patricia Cornelio-Krause says Stowell's "has the best Reubens and French Dip around." Of course, she may be a little biased: she's the genius behind TMK Baked Goods which provides all the sinful offerings on the dessert menu and the charcuterie dessert boards, as well as seasonal and holiday pleasers. Psst, the Reubens and French Dip really are the best around!

775 State Rd., 508-224-3320
stowellscafe.com

24

GO LOCAL
AT PLYMOUTH FARMERS MARKET

There's a lot to love about Plymouth's open-air Farmers Market. It's not just the seasonal fresh fruits and vegetables sourced from local farms; you'll also find savory fresh-baked pies and cranberry bread from Log Cabin Bakers, carrot-cake scones with maple glaze from Pies by Moira, and cranberry honey from Queen Bee Honey. You won't find such eclectic delicacies anywhere else. You can even pick up hand-dyed alpaca yarn and CapeLilly pumpkin spice soap. The Market is a community event, so prepare to see your friends and make new ones. And don't forget to bring the kids. They've got afternoon story time, and their Art on the Spot program will keep the little ones engaged. The Market also serves up soothing live music. Their new Plymouth Square location allows the Market to have even more room for the growing diversity of vendors.

101 Carver Rd.
plymouthfarmersmarket.org

TIP

Plymouth Farmers Market is open every Thursday 2:30–6 p.m. from May through October, rain or shine. From November through May, the market moves indoors. They support state SNAP and HIP programs, making healthy options available for all.

TASTE THE SMOKE
AT SURFSIDE SMOKEHOUSE

One of Plymouth's can't-miss restaurants is Surfside Smokehouse. Lori Luciani and Kim Hardy took ownership during the pandemic and had their grand opening in 2021. They added more seafood to the menu, but this is still a Southern BBQ joint and a great one, made even better by their amazing homemade sauces—choose gold! They offer traditional smokehouse fare including awesome Burnt End Sliders, The Big Pig Sandwich with pulled pork, lots of brisket choices, and of course—homemade pickles—a smokehouse staple. But don't snub the seafood. Their lobster roll is a monster, the lobster mac & cheese is devilishly rich, and the smoky clam chowder, with smoker jus added, is a must. Surfside's buck-a-shuck oyster happy hour is a big hit, and make sure to catch the live music and comedy shows. With two decks providing unmatched views of Plymouth Harbor, *Mayflower II*, and Plymouth Rock, a summertime vibe abounds.

14 Union St., 508-927-4111
surfsidesmokehouse.com

TIP

Surfside Smokehouse is advertised as the only waterfront Plymouth restaurant. Located next to Safe Harbor Marinas and literally hanging over the water, you won't find any restaurant closer to the sea!

CATCH YOUR BREATH
AT SECOND WIND BREWING COMPANY

What happens when three friends want to open a craft-beer brewery, but don't know how? Well, Second Wind Brewing Company owners Hans Terbush, Kenny Semcken, and J. R. Shepard decided the solution was to study the craft. The result: a wildly popular Howland Street taproom and beer garden with a social media following of over 20K! Second Wind is renowned for diverse IPAs and pale ales, specialty sours, darks, hard seltzers, lagers and wheats, and a steady lineup of new releases. You want creative? How about Fluffernutter Blackout: milk stout with marshmallow, peanut butter, chocolate, and vanilla bean! Second Wind's canned beers are available in nine different pubs and liquor stores from Plymouth to Boston. Join them for great holiday events like Oktoberfest, Halloween dog/people costume contests, Paint 'n' Sip gatherings, and Tarot Nights. Keep an eye on these guys: with the new upcoming Main Street location, they're just getting their second wind.

7 Howland St., 508-591-5915
secondwindbrewing.com

PAY A VISIT TO THESE OTHER CRAFT BREWERIES IN PLYMOUTH

Craft Beer Cellar Plymouth
44 Main St., 774-773-9229
craftbeercellar.com/plymouth

High Limb Cider
Village West Shopping Center, Carver Rd., 774-608-7428
highlimbcider.com

Independent Fermentations Brewing & Kombucha
127-3 Camelot Dr., 508-746-4634
independentfermentations.com

LlamaNama Beer Labs
49 Cordage Park Cir., 508-927-3260
llamanamabeerlabs.square.site

Sour Not Sorry Brewing
8a Court St.
sournotsorrybrewing.com

27

RAISE YOUR SPIRITS
AT DIRTY WATER DISTILLERY

Owner Pepi Avizonis and head distiller, Brenton MacKechnie, have a different approach to distilling spirits, and the result ain't your grandfather's whiskey, as they like to say. These master mixers—PhDs and chemists, mind you—celebrate the art and science of experimentation. Nothing is mass-produced here; their spirits are more like a bunch of hand-crafted one-offs you won't find elsewhere. Game to try bacon- or horseradish-infused vodka? How about gin made with juniper or cranberries? Ever tried beer whiskey? Arrive ready to experiment and armed with your "spirit" of adventure. Theirs is a true taproom, but it's not exactly old school. They serve their cocktails on tap, brewery style, and you can bring your own food—even your own dog if you want. It's about being comfortable. They offer live music and even metal embossing workshops. If you're looking for something different, with understated cool, visit Dirty Water.

49 Cordage Park Cir., Bay 2, 508-927-3260
dirtywaterdistillery.com

TIP

Join the team on Sunday mornings and Thursday evenings for the Dirty Water Run Club. It's an all-ability-levels group run, followed by a social hour in the taproom. They also team with Studio Uplift to hold yoga and POUND® classes right outside the Distillery offering a good way to make some new friends and work off those alcohol calories.

28

NURTURE YOUR SWEET TOOTH
AT FEDELE'S CHOCOLATES

Ron Fedele has spent the past 36 years crafting confectioneries. He opened Pembroke's Fedele's Chocolates in 1987 and won numerous awards for best chocolate shop on the South Shore. Since 2004, Fedele's Chocolates has sweetened Village Marketplace on Plymouth's waterfront. Their clusters, barks, truffles, turtles, fudge, white chocolate, and sugar-free options beckon from beneath the display glass and the beautifully boxed assortments quietly tempt you from the shelves. And if chocolate isn't your thing, the outside service window offers a wide selection of soft-serve ice cream. This family-owned shop makes you feel right at home, but if you can't get in to shop, enjoy their online "make your own" assortments—caramels, creams, dark chocolates, fruit slices, and more. Hands-on tours are available for kids in the Pembroke shop, where future chocolatiers help make the confections—and walk out with their creations!

170 Water St., Ste. 8, 508-746-8907
fedeleschocolates.com

29

FIND YOUR FLAVOR
AT TAVERN ON THE WHARF

Clustered within a mecca of harborside eateries—Lobster Hut, CabbyShack, Wood's Seafood, and Anna's Harborside Grille—Tavern on the Wharf rose from the ashes of the former Nix's to become one of Plymouth's favorite restaurants and entertainment spots. Just look for the iconic rooftop boat. Owner Paul Tupa opened Tavern on the Wharf in 2015 and restored it to a "family restaurant" more reminiscent of the former Weathervane. The menu is extensive, and the soups, salads, and appetizers are substantial enough to fill you up. But don't let that stop you from indulging in the entrées: savory fresh-caught seafood, burgers, steaks, tacos, coal-fired pizza, pasta, burrito and vegan bowls, and sandwiches. Favorite must-eats: pan-seared salmon, baked cod, tavern steak tips, fried calamari, and steak and cheese eggroll. Lots of live weekend music, from acoustic to country. They also host trivia nights, music bingo, comedy, and even an ugly Christmas sweater contest.

6 Town Wharf, 508-927-4961
tavernonthewharf.com

MUSIC AND ENTERTAINMENT

30

TAKE IN A SHOW
AT AMERICANA THEATRE COMPANY

You don't have to travel to Boston to experience outstanding theater productions. The Americana Theatre Company brings talented professional theater to the heart of downtown Plymouth. The company is the brainchild of South Shore native, Derek Martin, who started Americana as a summer theater in 2011. But under the leadership of Directors David and Erin Friday, Plymouth welcomed full-time community theater in 2015. The company has an impressive collection of full-time directors, designers, and actors whose stories teach, entertain, and inspire. Offerings have included 2023's well-received *Big Fish*, as well as *A Christmas Carol*, *The Three Musketeers*, *The 39 Steps*, and *It's a Wonderful Life*, all taking place at the beautiful Spire Center for the Performing Arts. The Americana Theatre Company also provides instructional training in performing arts, summer camps for budding actors, voice lessons, and musical training in piano, ukelele, flute, and percussion.

25½ Court St., 508-591-0282
americanatheatre.org

ADMIRE THE SPIRE

AT SPIRE CENTER FOR THE PERFORMING ARTS

If you're looking for a night of music, comedy, or stage performances, Spire Center for the Performing Arts is your place in downtown Plymouth. Housed in a historic 1880s-era Methodist church, this refurbished music hall offers a funky retro-chapel-y vibe with state-of-the-art light and sound. Board of Directors President Bob Hollis said on the Spire's website that the goal was to build "the best place to hear music anywhere," and they've followed through, attracting the best local and regional musical acts. The Greater Plymouth Performing Arts Center founded the Spire in 2012 and spearheaded efforts to fund its renovation. The result: a cozy venue, wonderful acoustics, and outstanding sight lines for its 225 lower-level seats and 50 balcony seats. And you're never more than 10 rows from the stage. The lower level features classrooms for stage performance education, a recording studio, and space for community activities.

25½ Court St., 508-746-4488
spirecenter.org

CATCH A PLAY
AT PRISCILLA BEACH THEATRE

For 86 years, the Priscilla Beach Theatre (PBT) has brought high-quality Summer Stock community theater to Plymouth. The oldest barn theater still in operation in the country, PBT is a boot camp for up-and-coming thespians who spend the summer living on the two-acre campus and perfecting their craft. On the brink of foreclosure in 2013, philanthropist Bob Malone and wife, Sandy, bought the rustic barn and completed an extensive, multi-million-dollar renovation. You'll experience a cozy and intimate 240-seat theater with great acoustics and sightlines. The 2023 Summer Stock season included *Singin' in the Rain*, *Beehive: the 60s Musical*, *Camelot*, and *Always . . . Patsy Cline*. Affectionately known as "Broadway in a Barn," PBT has a long and storied history, with Hollywood alumni Paul Newman, Rob Reiner, Dan Blocker, Peter Gallagher, and Jennifer Coolidge passing through its doors. PBT's mission also includes a focus on student workshops and providing theater training for children.

800 Rocky Hill Rd., 508-224-4888
pbtheatre.org

TIP

Priscilla Beach Theatre presents six theater shows from May to October with modest ticket prices ($37 per show). Enjoy free parking on the grounds.

33

VIEW THE STARS
AT BLAKE PLANETARIUM

If you haven't been to a planetarium since your fifth-grade science class field trip, you're in for a treat. The technology is truly out of this world! Blake Planetarium boasts the only 4K digital full dome outside of Boston as well as multichannel surround sound and high-res video that makes for an awesome experience. And while Blake Planetarium is still a school field trip destination, it offers a wide variety of entertaining and educational programming for all ages. Check out *Magic Treehouse: Space Mission* for the kids; *Destination Mars: The New Frontier*; the First Fridays series exploring the current night sky; and educational programs highlighting the nature of our solar system, matter, and whatever else that's out there! Best thing about it: the cost—$7 for all ages. Come to Blake Planetarium for state-of-the-art entertainment you won't get anywhere else on Earth . . . or the South Shore, anyway.

117 Long Pond Rd., 508-830-4470
facebook.com/blakeplanetarium

GO SOLO
WITH HISTORIC PLYMOUTH SELF-GUIDED WALKING TOUR

If you just don't have time for a scheduled group event, Historic Plymouth Self-Guided Walking Tour is for you. All you need is a smart phone. Purchase and download the Action Tour Guide app ($9.99) and your adventure begins. Starting at the Plymouth Visitor Center on Water Street, you'll follow the waterfront to Pilgrim Memorial State Park and learn about the Pilgrims' *Mayflower* voyage, Plymouth Rock's history, Cole's Hill and Chief Massasoit, Brewster Gardens, and the *Pilgrim Maiden* Statue. You'll also visit Burial Hill and the Plimoth Grist Mill Museum. What's cool is that the app's GPS knows where you are and adjusts the tour to match your pace. Enjoy the app's animated videos showing Plymouth from centuries past or its photos from inside the attractions. The tour lasts approximately an hour and covers about a mile on foot, so bring along some comfy shoes. You'll also need earbuds . . . and maybe sunscreen!

130 Water St., 508-506-1844
actiontourguide.com/place/
historic-plymouth-mayflower-self-guided-walking-tour

35

GREET A GHOST
ON PLYMOUTH NIGHT TOUR

If you're a ghost hunter, paranormal junkie, or just interested in a spooky night out, Plymouth Night Tour is for you. Local ghost-orian and storyteller, Geoff Campbell, will captivate you with tales of Plymouth's dark history, strange occurrences, ghost stories, murders, and encounters with fur-covered elemental spirits called pukwudgies, while strolling through the town's 17th-century streets and cemeteries. The walking tour takes about two hours, covering about a mile, and even includes a paranormal investigation. Campbell provides ghost hunter investigator tools for participants, including a K-II electromagnetic field meter. He also employs infrared cameras, and something called a Spirit Box—a modified transistor radio that scans white noise to pick up "otherworldly" communication. Each tour is different: sometimes the K-II meters light up, sometimes they don't—but that's the thrill of the hunt.

65 Main St., 508-927-2146
plymouthghosttours.com

DARE TO BRAVE THESE OTHER HAUNTING PLYMOUTH TOURS

Dead of Night Ghost Tours
31 North St., 508-277-2371
deadofnightghosttours.com

Spirit of Plymouth Walking Tours
"Murder, Mystery and Mayhem"
1 Cordage Ter., 508-517-8355
spiritofplymouth.com

TIP

In addition to being a ghost hunter, Campbell also leads the End Zone Militia at each New England Patriots home game, firing muskets after each touchdown! Maybe they could hire him to resurrect the ghosts of those Super Bowl–winning teams!

TAKE ADVANTAGE
OF SUMMER ON THE WATERFRONT

The Plymouth Waterfront is well-known for its restaurants and pubs, gift shops, ice cream, and scenic beauty. But its signature summer events elevate it to a New England destination. The Plymouth Waterfront Festival is one such event, drawing 15,000 people each August. It's a day packed with live music and entertainment, arts and crafts, a car show, and Plymouth's best food and drink. For weekly summer entertainment June through August, check out the Project Arts Summer Concert Series. Since 1996, fans have packed Pilgrim Memorial State Park's amphitheater Wednesdays at twilight for renowned musical acts like Kris Delmhorst, Average White Band, Jonathan Edwards, and Ritchie Havens, to name a few. And if you want to support a great cause, don't miss the two-day Thirsty Pilgrim Beer Festival in September. For 14 years, they've closed out the summer with the best in live music, beer tastings, and food while addressing food insecurity in Plymouth.

Water St.
plymouthwaterfrontfestival.com
projectarts.com
thethirstypilgrim.com

GET CREATIVE
AT PLYMOUTH CENTER FOR THE ARTS

Plymouth Center for the Arts is your one stop for art classes and workshops, summer art camps, events, and exhibits for both adults and children. The Center has been a vital creative asset to the downtown for over 50 years, introducing Plymouth residents to the region's burgeoning art scene as waterfront Tent Shows. Housed in their North Street gallery since 2008, Plymouth Center for the Arts offers opportunities to unleash your creative urges. Aching to toss clay against a potter's wheel? They can help. Have a hankering for origami? They've got a class. From drawing and sketching to watercolors and oil painting, talented and patient class instructors will bring out your inner Rembrandt. For kids, there's pottery, digital art classes, summer art camps, and art competitions held throughout the year. From May to October, their artisan shop stays open late to participate in First Fridays, offering live music and art exhibits.

11 North St., 508-746-7222
artsplymouth.org

DISCOVER
PLYMOUTH PHILHARMONIC ORCHESTRA

You don't need to travel to Boston to get your fix of classical music. The Plymouth Philharmonic Orchestra offers world-class performances with a roster of professionally trained, highly skilled musicians from around the globe. Flash in the pan? Not these guys. They've been providing an unmatched musical experience on the South Shore since 1913. But The Phil is orchestra 2.0, and not only includes classical, but contemporary and popular music. The 2023 season featured music from the *Harry Potter* films and tributes to Burt Bacharach, Tina Turner, and Aretha Franklin. The Phil is also an integral part of the America's Hometown Thanksgiving Celebration. Their educational outreach for the next generation is extensive. The Phil does all-ages concerts with hands-on instrument demos; school mini concerts with string, brass, and woodwind quartets; and programs that invite school choirs to perform with them. Enjoy one of Plymouth's true cultural gems.

116 Court St., 3rd floor, 508-746-8008
plymouthphil.org

LEND YOUR VOICE
TO PILGRIM FESTIVAL CHORUS

With performances featuring oratorios and major choral works, the Pilgrim Festival Chorus (PFC) brings moving vocal arrangements and a vibrant cultural livelihood to the Plymouth music scene. Founded in 1999, this all-volunteer, non-profit group features 80 local adult vocalists performing choral classics such as Mozart's *Requiem*, Handel's *Israel in Egypt*, and Brahms's *A German Requiem*. Each year, the chorale performs a winter concert highlighting seasonal/holiday favorites, a springtime major choral work accompanied by orchestra, and lighter pops-style summer programming. They also join in Plymouth Philharmonic Orchestra's Holiday Pops Concert. Led by artistic directors, Bill Richter and Elizabeth Chapman Reilly, PFC is dedicated to the mission of educating, enriching, and engaging their members and audiences through diverse choral works. In addition to holding open auditions each fall for aspiring vocalists, PFC offers two annual scholarships to South Shore High School graduating seniors pursuing collegiate musical studies.

pilgrimfestivalchorus.org

TIP

According to Board President, Sara Weiss, Pilgrim Festival Chorus may be rebranding in the coming year. So, keep an eye out for the "artists formerly known as PFC" and give them your unwavering support.

40

MAKE IT A NIGHT
AT NEW WORLD TAVERN

New World Tavern is synonymous with Plymouth entertainment. Owners Karl Heine and Roman Dombrowski have rocked the downtown since 2011, booking 70s/80s/90s cover bands, powerhouse female rockers, funk and soul musicians, hard rock and tribute bands, and heavy metal groups. For those who can belt out a tune, New World offers karaoke opportunities for prizes, and they even host their own version of *The Voice* competition. But that's just the music. Feel like a night of sipping and drawing? New World does that. Comedy? Trivia? Yep. How about dinner with a medium and messages from the great beyond? Check. New World also whips up great comfort food: pizzas, burgers, sliders, wraps, fish-and-chips, and mac & cheese, and they're famous for their craft beers—reds, browns, darks, ciders, IPAs, and wheats. After you've rocked the house Saturday night, join them for a hearty Sunday breakfast to soak up the libations.

56 Main St., 508-927-4250
thenewworldtavern.com

PAY A VISIT
TO PLYMOUTH MEMORIAL HALL

Plymouth Memorial Hall is not only a great place for live music; it's also much more. Sure, Bob Dylan put Memorial Hall on the map with his Rolling Thunder Revue in October of '75, but the Hall has been a community gathering spot since 1926. During WWII, the Hall hosted spaghetti suppers, movies, basketball games, and roller-skating nights that created a lasting sense of community. Today, the Hall still hosts community recreation programs, the Plymouth Holiday Market, the South Shore Food and Wine Expo, and is available for weddings, private parties, and corporate functions. But at night the 2,500-seat venue still rocks! The Hall books great acts like Blue Oyster Cult, 10,000 Maniacs, The Wallflowers, and The Mavericks, as well as nationally recognized cover bands like The Fab Four, Get the Led Out, and One Night of Queen. The Hall is also the place where the Plymouth Philharmonic Orchestra performs their America's Hometown Thanksgiving Celebration and the Hometown Holiday Show.

83 Court St., 508-747-1620 ext. 21100
memorialhall.com

GO FOR THE GRAIL
AT KING RICHARD'S FAIRE

Ever dream of being an extra in that *Monty Python and the Holy Grail* flick? Well, King Richard's Faire (KRF) is the next best thing. Join them each fall for their Renaissance Festival, where you can clutch a chicken bone in one hand and a goblet of mead in the other while watching live jousting, street performers, minstrels, wenches, aerial artists, and fire eaters. Got an old suit of armor in your closet? Get into the spirit and wear it. Or buy 16th-century garb from the talented artisans selling their wares. KRF is an all-ages event, with henna tattoo artists and face painting for the kids and tarot reading and pub crawls for the grown-ups. Make sure to participate in the themed weekend events like the Viking Tug O' War and the Adult Costume Contests including the bawdy Men in Kilts Contest, and the KRF Annual Cleavage Contest (must be 18 or over to participate).

235 Main St., Carver, 508-866-5391
kingrichardsfaire.net

TIP

The Renaissance Faire has been pleasing South Shore peasants for over 42 years. The Faire runs over eight weekends from the first week in September to the third week in October. Admission: Children under 3, free; children aged 4–11, $24; adults 12 and older, $43.

CATCH A TUNE
AT 1620 WINE BAR

The most successful Plymouth businesses do multiple things and do them well. 1620 Wine Bar is a great example. They are a restaurant serving tasty tapas, flatbreads, soups and salads, and creative boards. They are also an award-winning wine bar with a vast menu of hand-crafted wines bottled at their sister site, 1620 Winery at Cordage Park. And then there's the music. For the small-venue music fan, you won't find any better offerings than those in the Wine Bar's weekend lineup. The place is cozy and intimate, warm and inviting, and perfect for the singer-songwriters and acoustic musical acts they book, like Dylan Wheaton, Abigail Vail, Moonrise Duo, Ali Howshall, and Radio Honey. Speaking of multi-tasking, 1620 Winery at Cordage Park also coordinates wedding events, wedding showers, rehearsal dinners, corporate events, winery tours, and tastings in addition to comedy events, drag shows, formal galas, and wine pairing dinners—all accomplished with efficiency, taste, and the patron's wishes in mind!

170 Water St.
1620winebar.com

WATCH AN INDIE
AT PLIMOTH CINEMA

In the age of streaming, a movie theater might not seem like a must-visit, but the Plimoth Cinema is. If you're tired of CGI, explosions, and movie-related "universes," then Plimoth Cinema is worth a visit. It's the only arthouse cinema between Hingham and Dennis for experiencing indie and foreign films the big-box movie theater chains ignore. Located in the Henry Hornblower Visitor Center inside Plimoth Patuxet Museum, the Plimoth Cinema consists of two small theaters: the 110-seat Harriet K. Maxwell Theater and the 220-seat, ADA-compliant, Ruby Winslow Linn Theater. Both provide cozy and intimate theater experiences, perfect for a date night or quiet night out with friends. You can always get your concession standards—popcorn, candy, and fountain drinks—but on Saturdays, beer and wine are available from Mayflower Brewing Company. Start enjoying the movie experience again at Plimoth Cinema!

137 Warren Ave., 508-746-1622
plimoth.org/explore/cinema

45

CELEBRATE THE HOLIDAYS
AT EDAVILLE FAMILY THEME PARK

It's not hyperbole to say that a trip to the former Edaville Railroad was a major rite of passage for kids growing up on the South Shore. After years in limbo, Edaville Family Theme Park re-opened under new ownership in 2022, and while they have retained their classic steam-powered trains and vintage amusement park rides, they have shuttered the popular Thomas the Train and Dino Land attractions. Still, the park attracts large crowds with its cranberry bog train rides, Christmas Village, outdoor carousel, Big Eli Ferris Wheel, Tannenbaum Drop, Scrambler, Jolly Caterpillar, and mini-train and -rollercoaster rides, to name a few. Inside Ellis' Playhouse, bumper cars, an arcade, and model train room await the younger kids. Expect pricy theme-park food and merch, but their gift shop's vintage toys prove an unexpected treat. The park's still a great family option—and a sweet reminder of the Edaville of old.

5 Pine St., Carver, 508-866-8190
edaville.com

TIP

Edaville is no longer a year-round operation, focusing instead on the Christmas season. Operation periods in 2023 were from July 7–29 for their Christmas in July event and Festival of Lights from November 9–December 31.

SPORTS AND RECREATION

46

PERUSE THE PINES
AT MYLES STANDISH STATE FOREST

Since 1916, Plymouth County has preserved over 12,000 acres of state forest to benefit southeastern Massachusetts. Dozens of ponds and over 13 miles of paved and natural trails make Myles Standish State Forest ideal for outdoor recreation. For cycling fans, the paved riding roadways through the forest are unmatched, but be careful venturing onto the offroad hiking trails. Roots, stumps, rocks, and sandy patches have high-wipeout potential! Camping, hiking, horseback riding, swimming, birdwatching, and fishing are popular in the warm weather months. In winter, the forest trails are perfect for cross-country skiing, snowshoeing, or snowmobiling. Rare ecosystems and endangered animals and plants await. Glacial depressions formed 20,000 years ago shaped the landscape, creating such oddities as frost pockets, kettle hole ponds, and iron ore deposits. Special events such as guided hikes, cranberry bog tours, and a fishing derby are offered throughout the year, so check the website frequently for listings.

194 Cranberry Rd., Carver, 508-866-2526
mass.gov/locations/myles-standish-state-forest

47

HAVE A WHALE OF A TIME

ON CAPTAIN JOHN BOATS WHALE WATCH

If you're looking for adventure straight out of the Discovery Channel, it doesn't get any better than Captain John Boats Whale Watch. These four-hour cruises into Cape Cod Bay and Stellwagen Bank get you up close with some of the planet's most amazing creatures. And with a 99 percent success rate, you're sure to see native humpback, finback, pilot, minke, or even rare right whales. An on-site marine biologist will identify different whale species and answer your pressing questions. Hungry? Food and drink are available, too. Captain John Boats has been in business since 1946 operating out of Plymouth and Provincetown. In addition to whale watch tours, Captain John Boats offers deep sea fishing and several specialty cruises on their paddlewheel boat, the *Pilgrim Belle*, including harbor cruises, July 4th fireworks cruises, and sunset comedy cruises with adult beverages. Bring a jacket; it gets chilly out there on the bay.

10 Town Wharf, 508-556-1426
captjohn.com/whale-watch-plymouth

48

SOAK UP THE SUMMER SUN ON PLYMOUTH BEACHES

Plymouth boasts 37 miles of breathtaking coastline, but only has two public oceanside beaches—White Horse Beach and Plymouth Long Beach—three, if you count Brown's Bank. Whether it's two or three, Plymouth beaches are as beautiful as any on the east coast. Long beach is a three-mile barrier beach ideal for swimming, walking, and fishing. White Horse Beach is known for the historic Flag Rock a quarter mile offshore and its "shanty-town" houses in the sand that add to its funky vibe. Don't swim with the seals out there as great white sharks have been known to wander into Cape Cod Bay to snap them up. Plymouth has seen a kayaker or two bumped by those pesky predators, but that's nothing new in Massachusetts waters. The surf may be a bit cooler than the bathwater on Cape Cod, but you'll be thankful for it on an August day!

White Horse Beach: Taylor Ave.
Plymouth Long Beach: 1 Ryder Way
508-747-1620

TIP

Parking passes are required and cost $55 to access all beaches and ponds for the year. You'll have to shell out $75 for a 4x4 Beach Parking pass (if you want to travel over sand at Long Beach). Rates are scheduled to increase (surprise!) in 2024.

WALK THE JETTY
INTO PLYMOUTH HARBOR

Plymouth is awash in hiking trails, but have you ever tried hiking out into the middle of the ocean? The Plymouth Harbor Breakwater provides such an opportunity. The Jetty has been a popular attraction since 1971 when the Army Corps of Engineers completed the three-year breakwater project with its 219,000 tons of stone. After crossing the wooden footbridge, 1,400 feet of large flat boulders extend into the harbor before bending southeastward for another 2,100 feet. The stones' flat surfaces make the 1.2-mile round trip easy to navigate. But be careful! Deep gaps between stones could lead to a painful misstep. The cable rail spanning the distance can help guide the more cautious. Leave some "legal" graffiti if that's your thing, and don't worry, the saltwater washes it off. The Jetty is perfect for working off your downtown meal and offers waterfront and harbor views you won't find anywhere else.

PLYM-014A
seeplymouth.com/listing/plymouth-harbor-breakwall-the-jetty

MOTOR ON OVER
TO BROWN'S BANK

One of Plymouth's best kept secrets is Brown's Bank, located 100 yards off Plymouth Long Beach and only accessible by boat. The Bank's discovery in 1605 pre-dates the pilgrims, when Samuel de Champlain grounded his ship *Pinnace* on the future weekend party spot. Today, you'll find the Bank ringed with boats on summer weekends as crowds descend upon the white sand playground to throw frisbees, sunbathe, and play music. If you're hungry, it's a short wade to Cap'n Mike's Tiki Boat—think floating food truck—for hot dogs, shaved ice, ice cream, and adult beverages! Each year, winter storms and shifting sands create a different sandbar island, but its new shape never changes the festive atmosphere. And while ebbing tides often ground boats in the shallows, extending the day's fun is the only downside. By dusk, the tide comes in and Brown's Bank disappears, keeping its secret safe for another day.

facebook.com/brownsbankk

51

BEWARE
THE BRIDGEWATER TRIANGLE

Ever heard of the Bermuda Triangle? It's nothing compared to Massachusetts's own paranormal hotspot, the Bridgewater Triangle. The subject of centuries-old paranormal lore, the Triangle lies west of Plymouth and makes for a fun, spooky daytrip. The Triangle's three points lie in the towns of Abington (North), Rehoboth (Southwest), and Freetown (Southeast), with several additional towns lying within its 200 square-mile haunted boundaries. The largest freshwater swamp in Massachusetts, named Hockomock, or "place where spirits dwell" by the Wampanoag natives, also lies inside the Triangle's boundaries. Unearthed human artifacts date back more than 9,000 years. The Hockomock features sinkholes and quicksand, but over the years, reports of swirling lights, spectral fires, ghosts, unidentified animal-like creatures, and glowing orbs floating above water abound. Ghost hunters and paranormal enthusiasts blame the unnatural occurrences on the lingering spirits of both Native Americans and English colonists slaughtered during the 17th-century King Philip's War. So, venture into the Triangle if you dare.

TIP

Check out the Triangle hot-spots where paranormal activity has been reported, but keep in mind they are spread out over several towns: King Philip's Cave (Norton), The Lizzie Borden House in Fall River (where you can spend the night in Lizzie's room), Assonet Ledge in Freetown State Forest (Freetown), Anawan Rock (Rehoboth), Lake Nippenicket (Bridgewater), and the Mayflower Hill Cemetery (Taunton).

TAKE THE PLUNGE
AT WATER WIZZ WATER PARK

Water Wizz Water Park is the perfect summer destination for children of all ages, and the 20-minute drive south of Plymouth is well worth it. Water Wizz does a lot of things right, and maybe that's why they've been around since 1982. For the adventurous, don't miss the high-thrill, 76-foot-tall Devil's Peak water slide; psychedelic Pipeline Plunge; and 50-foot-tall Hurricane Hill. All will have you skipping along the water at crazy speeds. The slightly less death-defying tube rides include the super-fun Squid Row and Thunder Falls. For the squeamish, Mussel Beach wave pool and lazy river are an ideal solution to the summer heat, and you'll find plenty of shallow water splash pads for the young ones. Fun fact: Water Wizz was featured in two Hollywood movies: *Grown Ups* with Adam Sandler and David Spade in 2010 and *The Way, Way Back*, with Steve Carell in 2013.

3031 Cranberry Hwy., East Wareham, 508-295-3255
waterwizz.com

TIP

General admission prices aren't too bad: $48 for kids, $38 for adults and seniors. These prices drop to $34 and $29 after 2 p.m. Kids under 2 are always admitted for free. The food isn't cheap, so bring a thick wallet. Just don't get it wet.

RETURN TO NATURE
AT TIDMARSH WILDLIFE SANCTUARY

Tidmarsh Farms was once a family-owned, working cranberry bog, but in 2011, the land underwent a decade-long wetlands and stream "re-wilding" The results: Tidmarsh Wildlife Sanctuary, a 481-acre freshwater ecological restoration, the largest such project ever completed in the Northeast. Tidmarsh features seven trails varying in length from 1,400 feet to one mile, including an ADA compliant All Persons Trail. Each is perfect for birding, walking, and otherwise enjoying the Sanctuary's natural beauty and diverse wildlife. Tidmarsh also hosts Mass Audubon's school programming, a hands-on field or classroom experience for K–12 children that includes instructional sessions on bones and fossils, animal classification, trees and climate change, the food chain, storms, and habitats, just to name a few. For adults and families, the free Wednesday Walks educate about the diverse plant and animal species in the area. Tidmarsh is off limits to dogs, bicycling, horseback riding, camping, and fishing in order to maintain the delicate ecosystem in the Sanctuary, so please be respectful of this unique environment.

60 Beaver Dam Rd., 508-927-1200
massaudubon.org/places-to-explore/wildlife-sanctuaries/tidmarsh

54

BRAVE THE BOGS
AT RED MEADOW FARM

Relative newcomers to the business, Jordan and Equus Trundy have embraced cranberry farming with a passion at Red Meadow Farm. They also share their love of the berry with the curious—and adventurous. Join them for Bog Tours and learn about how their cranberries are grown and harvested. You can also don some rubber chest waders for the Wade in the Bog Harvest Event and get up close and personal with the floating berries. Don't worry, Jordan and Equus will be right there beside you. But Red Meadows isn't just Agri-Tourism, their farm stand features homegrown cranberries, blackberries, raspberries, blueberries, apples, pears, and veggies. They partner with farms from the six New England states to feature sustainably grown and produced syrups, coffees, honey, and other delectables to celebrate the region's family farms. Give them a visit and pick up one of their Red Meadows sweatshirts, hats, or tees while you're at it.

213 Meadow St., Carver, 508-500-1001
redmeadow.net/events

TIP

Bog Tours run $15–$20; the Wade in the Bog Harvest Event runs $60–$75. Not feeling flush? Check out their Instagram page to get a real sense of life on a cranberry bog. From harvesting berries to learning about the snakes, turtles, and frogs that inhabit the land, it's an education.

55

HIT THE SEAS

FOR MONOMOY ISLAND EXCURSIONS

While Monomoy Island Excursions is not exactly a Plymouth adventure, it's something everyone who respects the ocean's amazing ecosystem should experience. Monomoy Island is an eight-mile-long barrier beach off Chatham, home to the largest gray seal population on the US Atlantic coast. Monomoy Island Excursions puts you on a 43-foot Coast Guard–certified boat to witness up to 50,000 of these playful acrobats gliding through the narrow shoreline channels or basking in the sun along the beach. You will also see different species of seabirds and the occasional great white shark patrolling the shores looking for a snack. The boat is roomy and comfortable, and a trained naturalist is available to narrate the tour and answer your questions. The tour also passes through Harwich Port's Wychmere Harbor and gives you a close-up of Chatham's Stage Harbor Lighthouse and Monomoy Lighthouse. Keep a lookout for Chatham Lighthouse in the distance.

731 MA-28, Harwich Port, 508-430-7772
monomoysealcruise.com

TIP

The 75-minute tour costs $45 for adults, $40 for children (4–12 years), and $20 for infants (3 years and younger). Private charters for weddings, birthdays, or corporate functions are available.

RELEASE YOUR INNER VIKING

AT LONG HOUSE AXE THROWING

If you haven't tried axe throwing yet, what are you waiting for? Experience the rush at Long House Axe Throwing in downtown Plymouth. The day's frustrations will melt away when you rear back and throw, hearing that "clunk" of metal as it pierces the wood. The sport requires form and accuracy—not necessarily strength—so axe throwing isn't just for lumberjacks. Viking Trainers roam the floor and help everyone, skilled or unskilled, improve their game. Long House also offers knife throwing as part of their urban, weapon-tossing lineup. Come work off stress and enjoy an awesome roster of craft beers from local breweries like the Mayflower and Second Wind Brewing Companies. Long House runs sanctioned axe- and knife-throwing leagues throughout the year and is the perfect stop for corporate team-building events, birthdays, or bachelor/bachelorette parties. You must be 18 years or older to throw. Teens 15–17 years old may throw with adult supervision.

46 Main St., 508-747-7700
longhouseaxethrowing.com

57

MAKE A SPLASH
AT NELSON MEMORIAL PARK

The great thing about Plymouth is that you can take your kids to the park and have a spectacular ocean view at the same time. Nelson Memorial Park is a 3.9-acre green space just down the street from the busy waterfront, providing benches and a large grassy area in which to relax, unwind, or throw a frisbee. The Park underwent an extensive renovation in 2010, including upgrades to the playground infrastructure which features swing sets, climbing structures, and slides. There's also a concession stand and picnic area, a one-mile bike path along the harbor to North Plymouth, and an amazing splash pad for the kids. Oh, did I mention the boat ramp for canoes and kayaks? What's best is at low tide the kids can walk out into the ocean for 100 yards, search for shells, and barely get their feet wet. Parking is limited, but it's free. In Plymouth, that's a win!

255 Water St., 508-747-1620 ext. 10137
seeplymouth.com/listing/nelson-memorial-park

58

RIDE THE SKINNIES
AT PINE HILLS MOUNTAIN BIKING TRAILS

Pine Hills Mountain Biking Trails are a mountain biker's paradise, with 160 wooded trails totaling 69 miles, and a total descent of over 9,700 feet. Pine Hills sits to the north (nuclear power plant side) and south (Serious Cycles bike shop side) of Route 3A and isn't for the faint of heart. The black diamond trails are loaded with serious jump lines, skinnies, rickety ramps leading up and over dangerous rock formations, tight turns, and a sweet teeter-totter. The fast-moving, narrow, and winding trails slalom through thick pines that tickle the edges of the handlebars, so don't forget a helmet and pads. All trails are unsanctioned, so ride at your own risk! If you think you have the right stuff, don't miss the One-Up and Maneater (Serious Cycles side) and Temple of Doom, Save a Buck, and Shady Acres (nuclear side). There are also numerous green and blue trails for the novice mountain biking enthusiasts.

TIP

Parking is available directly across the street from Serious Cycles on Route 3A at Cleft Rock Parking lot. The trails south of 3A tend to be more difficult as they were dirt bike trails and include very steep and/or sandy patches. For a visual walkthrough of several Pine Hills black diamond trails, check out "JC Trails" on YouTube.
youtube.com/watch?v=4NZUh2UIaDA

HIT THE WATER
AT BILLINGTON SEA KAYAK

One of the best ways to experience Plymouth's waters is to glide across them in a kayak, canoe, or stand-up paddle board. You won't find a better bunch than the experts at Billington Sea Kayak to get you equipped to do just that. Thirty-seven years in the business is worth something, and they are hands-down the most respected shop in the area. If you're just looking for a daytrip adventure, their equipment rentals will get you right into the action. They are situated right beside Billington Sea, a 270-acre watery playground with five miles of shoreline and numerous wildlife opportunities—bald eagles, osprey, great blue heron, red-bellied turtles, and two secluded islands open to the public. If you're looking to buy, owner Doug Gray will let you test-drive your kayak or canoe before deciding to purchase. They are five minutes from downtown Plymouth and provide select instructional classes during the summer months.

41 Branch Point Rd., 508-746-5644
billingtonseakayak.com

60

EXPLORE THE WILD
WITH WILDLANDS TRUST

Wildlands Trust is a conservation organization that has protected native habitats in southeast Massachusetts for the past 50 years. The result: public access to some of the most scenic forests, wetlands, and coastal areas in New England. The Trust has worked to protect land in over 12 southeastern communities. In Plymouth, these include the Davis-Douglass Conservation Area, comprising three large land preserves of over 220 acres to the east of Long Pond; Halfway Pond Conservation Area which covers 400 acres of wildlands and preserves north and northwest of Halfway Pond; Shifting Lots Preserve, a saltwater marsh on the southern end of Ellisville Harbor State Park; and South Triangle Pond Conservation Area, consisting of 47 acres of pinelands and pond shores between Cooks Pond and South Triangle Pond. These magnificent, tranquil areas are ideal for hiking, cycling, fishing, canoeing, and birdwatching. So, get out and experience Plymouth's green spaces, a gift that will stand for generations.

675 Long Pond Rd., 774-343-5121
wildlandstrust.org/plymouth

HIT THE LINKS
AT SOUTHERS MARSH GOLF COURSE

Golf aficionados may question this selection, asking, "What about Pinehills or Waverly Oaks?" True, these are some of the best public golf courses in New England, but those aren't situated on a 100-year-old working cranberry bog. And for those who don't want a prolonged golfing experience, a par-61 executive course like Southers Marsh—with 11 par-threes and 7 par-fours—might be the ticket. Southers Marsh is incredibly scenic, but be warned: you may lose a ball or two in the bogs. The fairways and greens are always in great shape and the golf season extends into December and beyond. If you just want to hit balls and grab a beer or two, head over to The Barn. With 10 hitting bays and TopTracer technology, you can compete against your friends or play simulations on golf courses around the world. They don't rent clubs, so make sure to bring your own.

30 Southers Marsh Ln., 508-830-3535
southersmarsh.com

TIP

Southers Marsh runs seasonal golf leagues, senior leagues, and tournaments. When it gets too cold and snowy on the course, a winter golf league is held in The Barn. For a good laugh, don't miss the Southers Marsh commercials posted on their website.

OTHER PUBLIC GOLF COURSES IN PLYMOUTH

Pinehills Golf Club
54 Clubhouse Dr., 508-209-3000
pinehillsgolf.com

Waverly Oaks Golf Club
444 Long Pond Rd., 508-224-6700
waverlyoaksgc.com

Crosswinds Golf Club
424 Long Pond Rd., 508-830-1199
golfcrosswinds.com

Atlantic Country Club
450 Little Sandy Pond Rd., 508-759-6644
atlanticcountryclub.net

Squirrel Run Golf Club
32 Elderberry Dr., 508-746-5001
golfatsquirrelrun.com

Village Links Golf Club
265 South Meadow Rd., 508-830-4653
golfatsquirrelrun.com

GET YOUR GOAT
AT BEAWELL WITH GOAT YOGA

Looking for the G.O.A.T. exercise? Well, Beawell with Goat Yoga may just be the thing. Goat yoga has been a "thing" for a few years now, and this form of animal therapy lowers anxiety and blood pressure while fulfilling the exercise benefits and mindfulness of yoga. Beatrice Whalin, owner of Caregiver, Acupressure, Yoga & Reiki Therapy creates a relaxing atmosphere with singing bowls, sunshine, and adorable goats—and who hasn't wished for a goat to stand on their back just once? Beawell with Goat Yoga is a collaboration between Whalin and Rebecca Roberts of Hidden Gem Homestead, who supplies the adorable bleaters. Together, they provide a family-friendly entertaining afternoon that's "goat" for the body and soul. Beawell has arranged goat yoga at birthday parties and bachelorette parties, as well as Mother's and Father's Day celebrations! You can also join Whalin for Full-Moon Beach Yoga at Nelson Park in Plymouth.

170 Court St., 781-789-8782
facebook.com/beatrice5079

REWARD THE KIDS
WITH OFF THE WALL KIDZ

When your little ones are bored with the museums, attractions, and shopping, give them a treat at Off the Wall Kidz. Located 15 minutes west of Plymouth, Off the Wall Kidz is an indoor playground created from a child's perspective. They'll love the enclosed climbing structure with walkways and bridges; the arcade and interactive games; the pretend city with a fire station, doctor's office, and grocery store (with carts!); the ball pit with 25,000 colored balls; the interactive projector slide; and the trampolines. For kids five years and under, the Toddler area is perfect with a padded play space and soft play toys, a merry-go-round swing, and spinning seats. This family-owned business prioritizes safety, and the staff continually sanitizes equipment. The ball pit even has its own dedicated sanitizing machine! Off the Wall Kidz provides private birthday party rooms, but it is also possible to rent out the entire 10,000 square foot space for your own private mega play date.

160 N Main St., Carver, 888-808-5633
offthewallkidz.com

TIP

Off the Wall Kidz is geared toward children 2–8, but pre-teens are also welcome. An all-day pass is $13–$17 depending on age, and adults are always admitted for free. However, plan to shell out a pricey $399 when booking a birthday party or private play.

FAITH
NATIONAL MONUMENT TO THE FOREFATHERS
ERECTED BY A GRATEFUL PEOPLE IN REMEMBRANCE OF THEIR LABORS, SACRIFICES AND SUFFERINGS FOR THE CAUSE OF CIVIL AND RELIGIOUS LIBERTY.

CULTURE AND HISTORY

RESURRECT THE PAST
AT PLIMOTH PATUXET MUSEUMS

The Plimoth Patuxet Museums are an immersive journey into early 17th-century life, with major exhibits including *Mayflower II*, Plimoth Grist Mill Museum, Craft Center, Historic Patuxet, and the Seventeenth-Century English Village. The latter two are true living museums, reflecting the coexistence of the Native Wampanoag and English colonists in the original 1620 Plimoth Colony. Step back in time to walk through the colonists' reconstructed homes, gardens, and two-story fort with replica cannons, or visit the Wampanoags' dome-shaped wetus and help them hollow out a mishoon for the river. Skilled interpreters, dressed in period attire, demonstrate historical activities such as farming, cooking, and crafts, while sharing insights about 17th-century life. The museum began modestly with two homes on the waterfront in 1947 but added *Mayflower II*—a replica of the original ship—in 1957 and the English settlement in 1959. Historic Patuxet was added in 1973.

137 Warren Ave., 508-746-1622
plimoth.org

TIP

Once known as Plimoth Plantation, Plimoth Patuxet museums are one of the most popular field trips in the state and include interactive workshops. Online distance learning with museum educators and overnight visits for the kids are also available.

CLIMB ABOARD

MAYFLOWER II

With its intricate rigging, four towering masts, six sails, and weathered wooden hull, *Mayflower II* faithfully recreates the original vessel that carried the Pilgrims from Plymouth, England, to Plymouth, Massachusetts, in 1620. Since June 1957, when *Mayflower II* arrived in Plymouth, over 25 million people have ventured on deck to explore the floating museum. Following a three-year absence from Plymouth for a full restoration to prepare for Plymouth's 400th anniversary, *Mayflower II* returned to Plymouth in August of 2020. At 106 feet long and 25 feet wide, it is surprisingly small, and raises the question of how 102 passengers and 30 crew could have lived comfortably aboard for up to nine months—including the treacherous 66-day Atlantic journey. Unfortunately, accessibility is an issue. The ship's authenticity creates difficult stair climbs and steep inclines made more treacherous by potential sea swells, but if you are able, the experience makes it well worth the trip.

Plymouth Waterfront, 508-746-1622
plimoth.org/plan-your-visit/explore-our-sites/mayflower-ii

TIP

No one is exactly sure what happened to the original *Mayflower*. In 1624, a value assessment was performed, but no maritime record of the ship exists after that. A 2017 book—*The Mayflower* by R. Fraser published by St. Martin's Press—reveals that the ship was most likely sold for scrap.

LEARN THE LEGEND

OF PLYMOUTH ROCK

Okay, we all know that Plymouth Rock is a bit underwhelming as far as monuments go. There, I said it. But it's important to view the Rock through the lens of what it represents—the foundation upon which America was settled. In that sense, the Rock as a symbol is anything but underwhelming. The Rock started out at least three times larger than what sits under the Water Street portico today. It broke in two during the move to the town square in 1774. In 1867, the Rock's base was trimmed to fit the first granite canopy constructed above it, and much was lost to souvenir seekers chipping away at it throughout the years. The top of the stone was relocated twice more, to Pilgrim Hall in 1834 and finally to the current harbor location in 1880 where it was reunited with the base.

79 Water St.
seeplymouth.com/listing/plymouth-rock

TIP

Whether Plymouth Rock was truly the place the Pilgrims first set foot in the new world is unlikely, given that it wasn't identified as such until 1741. Not to mention, it has been established that the Pilgrims landed in Provincetown a month before arriving in Plymouth.

LEAVE A TOKEN
AT SACRIFICE ROCK

A lesser-known Plymouth protuberance, but just as significant in native Wampanoag history, is Sacrifice Rock. Acquired and maintained by the Plymouth Antiquarian Society since 1928, Sacrifice Rock may be the oldest of Plymouth's historic sites, existing hundreds of years before the Pilgrims' arrival. For centuries, natives passing through Plymouth would leave sticks, leaves, or small stones on the Rock to ensure safe passage on their journey or as a token of sacrifice, although the true function of "God's Rock"—as inscribed on its plaque—has been lost to history. Today, the Rock rests in a small pocket park on Old Sandwich Road, nestled at the wood's edge beside a modern residential development. Unlike the other, more famous Rock, there's no ostentatious portico covering it and there is never a crowd surrounding it. But visitors will still observe that the Rock is still frequently adorned with stones and tokens that honor the Wampanoag spiritual traditions.

394 Old Sandwich Rd.
seeplymouth.com/listing/sacrifice-rock

68

MOUNT

THE MAMMOTH PULPIT ROCK

Okay, so you want to see a REAL rock? Motor on over to Clark's Island in Duxbury Bay to view Pulpit Rock. The glacial boulder is a monster, at least 20 times larger than Plymouth Rock. And it isn't hidden behind gates or ropes. Anyone can touch it, climb on it, or appreciate its grandeur up close. Unlike Plymouth Rock, Pulpit Rock is the site of an actual historical event, one exemplifying the Pilgrims' powerful religious convictions. On Sunday, December 8, 1620, in Plymouth Harbor, 18 men set off from the *Mayflower* to reach the new world but found themselves marooned on Clark's Island. After fixing their boat, they held a church service and rested instead of venturing the short distance to their ultimate destination. For the Pilgrims, reaching the new world—the place they had crossed an ocean to reach—took a backseat to honoring the Sabbath.

Clark's Island, Duxbury

CELEBRATE THE ARTS
WITH FIRST FRIDAYS PLYMOUTH

The Plymouth Bay Cultural District was established in 2014 to highlight downtown Plymouth's vibrant art and culture. The largest of more than 50 Cultural Districts in Massachusetts, Plymouth boasts art galleries, music venues, coffee shops, restaurants, historical landmarks, and small businesses with a one-of-a kind energy. On the first Friday of each month, the District features an eclectic mix of entertainment and art from the area's most talented craftspeople. You'll experience live art demonstrations and stunning pottery, glass, jewelry, paintings, and wearables from participating studios and galleries, along with live music. Plymouth's rich history is also on display as the historic Hedge House, Howland House, and Spooner House open their doors to the public. Restaurants and pubs are jumping, and the galleries host exciting activities for kids and adults. Experience First Fridays and meet the talented creatives in your community. The events are free, starting up in May and going through to the end of October (5 p.m.–8 p.m.).

Downtown Plymouth, 774-608-5040
firstfridaysplymouth.com

70

SCOUR THE EPITAPHS
ON BURIAL HILL

Burial Hill is one of the oldest cemeteries in the country and final resting place for many original *Mayflower* passengers. At 165 feet above sea level, the five-acre plot combines spectacular ocean views with a somber sense of peace and reverence. Once the site of the Old Pilgrim Fort and Meeting House, Burial Hill became an internment site in 1680—although many buried there are likely to have died earlier. Take time to peruse the heartfelt epitaphs, especially those for children like Alma May Butler (December 17, 1888): "Her heart was folded deeply in ours." The graveyard is a haven for iconography, such as winged skulls, hourglasses, willows and urns, clasped hands, sheafs of wheat, winged cherubs, and lambs. Some notable gravestones among the more than 2,000 that make up the cemetery landscape include William Bradford, the first Governor of Plymouth; Squanto, a Patuxet tribe member and friend to the colonists; and Mary Allerton, the last *Mayflower* survivor.

School St.
plymouthantiquarian.org/burial-hill

TIP

To learn more about Burial Hill's iconography, visit the Plymouth Antiquarian Society's website for interesting videos (plymouthantiquarian.org/burial-hill/iconography). They also provide tours of the cemetery. For a historical record of the Burial Hill tombstone epitaphs, check out *Epitaphs from Burial Hill, Plymouth, Massachusetts, from 1657 to 1892* housed in the Library of Congress (loc.gov).

71

LINE THE STREETS
FOR AMERICA'S HOMETOWN THANKSGIVING CELEBRATION

For 28 years, America's Hometown Thanksgiving Celebration has provided a weekend of memorable events, music, and entertainment for the entire family. A Friday night concert featuring the Plymouth Philharmonic kicks off the festivities at Memorial Hall. Saturday's main event is the morning parade along Water Street, voted number one Thanksgiving parade in the country. The procession showcases local marching bands and spectacular floats presented chronologically, highlighting not only the Pilgrims' experience but also historical events throughout the country's 400-year history. Indulge in the offerings from food trucks and the all-day Beer & Wine Garden throughout the day. Kids will love the Children's Pavilion with face painting, art, and physical activities. Enjoy the Historic Village with period re-enactors and interpreters—something Plymouth excels at—and amazing pottery, ironware, and crafts in the Artisan Marketplace. Rounding out the weekend is the Saturday evening Memorial Hall concert and a Sunday Harvest Market with local vendors.

Water St.
usathanksgiving.com

TIP

Although the parade is free and open to the public, the Friday and Saturday night concerts will run $30–$35. The Beer & Wine Garden requires $5 to enter. If you can't make it to Plymouth, you can watch the parade on WCVB Boston's live streaming and on-demand platform. The parade also airs nationally in select markets across Hearst Television stations.

72

CLIMB TO THE TOP
AT MYLES STANDISH MONUMENT STATE RESERVATION

The Myles Standish Monument rests 200 feet above sea level on Captain's Hill in Duxbury in Plymouth County and honors the military leader of the Plimoth Colony. As an active soldier, Standish defended the colonists against natives and other threats for more than 20 years. Built in 1872, the monument features a 14-foot-tall *Myles Standish* statue perched atop a 116-foot base and tower. Stairmaster devotees won't mind tackling the 125 granite steps to witness panoramic views of the South Shore, but the rest of us may want to pace ourselves. While some question the monument's relevance due to Standish's brutal tactics against natives, it's hard to argue against his role in the Plimoth Colony's survival. Wooded trails surrounding the monument are perfect for walking and cycling, and picnic tables offer a scenic respite in summer months. The monument is open from Memorial Day to Labor Day.

Crescent St., Duxbury, 508-747-5360
mass.gov/locations/myles-standish-monument-state-reservation

73

GO MILES
TO GLIMPSE MYLES (STANDISH'S LEGS)

Had enough of Myles Standish, yet? Well, this half-statue in Plymouth County doesn't have enough of him—just his legs. And how do we know they're Myles Standish's legs? In 1922, lightning struck the 50-year-old Myles Standish Monument in Duxbury and poor Myles bore the brunt of the strike. All that was left were the singed legs, although rumor has it the intact head is somewhere in Massachusetts. The legs were salvaged from a Quincy quarry in the 1990s and now reside in Halifax resident Marc Valentine's front yard. The cool thing about this half-embodied statue: Mr. Valentine often comes out to meet with curious leg-gawkers, regaling them with stories and history, and sharing historical artifacts. So, shake a leg and visit Marc and Myles to enjoy some alternative Plymouth history. Admission is half-off—see what I did there?—actually, admission is free, but Mr. Valentine welcomes donations.

20 Dwight St., Halifax

74

GET FIRED UP FOR JULY 3RD

ON MANOMET BEACH

Nothing screams summer like July 3rd on Manomet Beach, a truly organic, unscripted, and patriotic evening of organized chaos. Bonfires, explosives, and late-night revelry mark this pre-Independence Day event, pitting neighborhood against neighborhood in a quest for the best impromptu fireworks display along a miles-long stretch of beach. The event is rooted in tradition and has been held on local neighborhood beaches since the 1800s. The celebration attracts the entire town, so it's best to arrive early for a good seat along the bluff. Flames light the sky; sparklers and glow-stick jewelry imbue the darkness with pre-patriotic fervor; American flags fly; and red, white, and blue duds adorn the revelers. The action begins after sunset when the explosives are ignited. Despite the potential for mishaps—the fun doesn't start until a stray firework scatters the crowds—the risk-benefit ratio is slightly in your favor.

Manomet Beach

TIP

A YouTube song by Tedd Rodman, "Manomet (On the 3rd of July)," has immortalized the local event. Check it out here: youtube.com/watch?v=CJyH0ysSX-g

75

HONOR THE SACRIFICE
AT PARTING WAYS CEMETERY

Named for a 94-acre settlement near the Plymouth/Kingston line, Parting Ways Cemetery is a tiny burial plot surrounded by a white fence and stone border. It's the resting place for four formerly held slaves and Revolutionary War soldiers: Prince Goodwin, Quamony Quash, Cato Howe, and Plato Turner. If you thought the soldiers of the 54th Massachusetts Regiment from the 1989 Civil War–film, *Glory*, were the first Black soldiers, think again. The decision on which side to fight a century earlier during the Revolutionary War was complicated for Black people. For enslaved Blacks, including Quamony Quash, the British dangled the prospect of freedom in exchange for military service. Former slaves had to choose to fight for the country that enslaved them or the opposition. Because more than 80 percent of Black soldiers fought for the British, Parting Ways is a reminder of those who forgave past transgressions and sacrificed personal freedom for their country.

Plympton Rd.
plymouthantiquarian.org/2020/06/19/visit-parting-ways

76

PLAN A VISIT
TO PLYMOUTH LIGHT STATION

Another of New England's grand lighthouses, Gurnet Light was built on 27 majestic, ocean-front acres on the northeast entrance to Plymouth Bay in 1768. Gurnet Light started service as a house with twin lanterns on either end. It was damaged in the Revolutionary War, burned to the ground in 1801, and rebuilt as twin lighthouses in 1803. The towers were rebuilt again in 1843. The northeast lighthouse was dismantled in 1924, and the remaining structure, standing 39 feet tall and rising 102 feet above the sea, is the oldest free-standing, wooden lighthouse operating in the United States. It also housed the first female lighthouse keeper, Hannah Thomas, from 1776–1790. Cliff erosion has threatened the Gurnet, forcing the town to move it 140 feet back from the bluff in 1998. The non-profit Project Gurnet & Bug Lights, Inc., manages the property and seeks to permanently acquire the lighthouse through the National Historic Lighthouse Preservation Act.

Gurnet Point, Plymouth Bay
buglight.org

TIP

Plymouth Light Station also houses the historic Fort Andrew, which was in service during both the Revolutionary and Civil Wars. The two historic sites rest on private, government land and are only open to the public during Duxbury's Opening of the Bay Festival in May. Tours can also be arranged through Project Gurnet & Bug Lights, Inc.

77

GIVE A SALUTE
TO FLAG ROCK

You can't miss Flag Rock—a massive boulder rising from the surf with an American flag painted on its surface—when making the turn from White Horse Road to Taylor Avenue or relaxing on White Horse Beach. Jumping off the northern edge of Flag Rock has been a childhood rite of passage for decades, but few know the rock's history. In 1940, six Plymouth teens painted the American flag to cover up a German swastika. It was World War II, and German U-Boats patrolled the coast. Plymouth lore has it that German sailors painted the swastika to taunt the locals. But brothers Paul, Donald, and Lawrence Deary along with three other patriotic teenagers took back their beach with a paint can. When the six teenagers enlisted after Pearl Harbor, residents continued splashing Flag Rock with a fresh coat of paint each year, a tradition still alive and well in 2024.

White Horse Beach, Taylor Ave.

"CHECK OUT" HERRING POND WAMPANOAG TINY LIBRARY

Don't you love those tiny libraries with glassed-in cabinets and books for the taking? It's the ultimate in sharing and repurposing, gifting free entertainment, education, and knowledge within a community. But you haven't seen anything until you've seen the Herring Pond Wampanoag tiny library. A partnership among the Plymouth Public Library, Community Art Collaboration, and the Herring Pond Wampanoag Tribe created this forward-thinking community resource. There aren't just books in those beautiful artisan-built, honeycomb compartments. You'll find seeds for people to grow their own food, canned goods for the hungry, and books sharing Wampanoag culture from indigenous authors. The library also addresses digital equity. Those without internet connectivity can simply park in the Herring Pond Wampanoag Meetinghouse parking lot and use WiFi for free. Enjoy—and support—this amazing collaboration to help share Wampanoag culture and assist the community.

128 Herring Pond Rd., 508-304-5023

STEP INSIDE
THE JABEZ HOWLAND HOUSE

The Jabez Howland House holds the distinction as the only Plymouth residence directly connected to *Mayflower* Pilgrims. Jabez Howland, the eighth child of John and Elizabeth Howland, purchased the home in 1669 and lived there until 1680. John Howland died in 1672, so it is likely he and Elizabeth, original Pilgrims who sailed on the *Mayflower*, spent time there. The home has been added onto throughout the years and the displays include numerous items from 17th- and 18th-century life: a spinning wheel; finger bowls; original stone floors; wood ceiling beams; a toaster, crane, and bake-oven within the hearth; an infant's crib; letters written by Jabez Howland; and artifacts from John Howland's Rocky Nook (Kingston) property. The residence was a private home until its purchase as a museum in 1912, but a renovation in 1940 restored it to its original appearance. The house is open from mid-June through late October.

33 Sandwich St., 508-746-9590
pilgrimjohnhowlandsociety.org/the_jabez_howland_house

TIP

John Howland was actually swept from the *Mayflower*'s deck into high seas but was miraculously pulled back aboard. The Pilgrim John Howland Society runs the Jabez Howland House. Admission is $6 for adults, $5 for seniors and military, $2 for children 6–12 years, and free for Plymouth residents and children under 2 years.

OTHER HISTORIC PLYMOUTH HOUSES

The 1640 Richard Sparrow House
42 Summer St., 508-747-1240
sparrowhouse.com

The 1677 Harlow House
119 Sandwich St., 508-746-0012
plymouthantiquarian.org/historic-sites/harlow-house

The 1749 Spooner House
27 North St., 508-746-0012
plymouthantiquarian.org/historic-sites/spooner-house

The 1809 Hedge House
126 Water St., 508-746-0012
plymouthantiquarian.org/historic-sites/hedge-house

80

MARVEL
AT NATIONAL MONUMENT TO THE FOREFATHERS

The National Monument to the Forefathers, at 81 feet high, is thought to be the country's largest freestanding granite monument. But despite its imposing presence, what the Monument represents is even grander. Five statues adorn the tower, representing virtues the Pilgrims held dear. The statue, *Faith*, stands at the top, clutching the Bible and pointing toward heaven. On the lower tier sits statues representing *Morality*, *Law*, *Education*, and *Liberty*, principles upon which the Pilgrims founded the nation. Four large panels grace the structure, two of which list the names of each passenger on the *Mayflower* and another stating: "Erected by a grateful people in remembrance of their labors, sacrifices, and suffering for the cause of civil and religious liberty." Built over the course of 30 years and completed in 1889, the Monument was planned at 150 feet, but scaled back due to cost restrictions during the Civil War.

72 Allerton St., 508-747-5360
mass.gov/locations/national-monument-to-the-forefathers

LEARN THE ROPES
AT PLYMOUTH CORDAGE MUSEUM

The Plymouth Cordage Museum pays homage to "Plymouth's other history" as Museum Director, Lucile Leary, told *Wicked Local* in 2021—one that shaped modern Plymouth. Located on the original Plymouth Cordage Company site, this unassuming museum contains over 30,000 fascinating historical images and artifacts from the world's most successful rope and twine manufacturer and the largest Plymouth employer for over a century. Observe rope samples, centuries-old tools and miniatures, and grooved floors bearing the company's 140 years of wear and tear (1824–1965). Learn about Cordage's visionary founder, Bourne Spooner, who created a welcoming community for his diverse immigrant workforce that included free day care, housing, universal health care, nutrition programs, schools, a library, and a gymnasium. The company fielded sports teams and even had their own newspaper. The museum may not have the cache of others in town, but it serves as a reminder of the possibilities of forward thinking.

10 Cordage Park Cir., 774-454-9945
plymouthcordageco.org

PIECE TOGETHER THE PAST

AT PILGRIM HALL MUSEUM

Pilgrim Hall Museum is the country's oldest continually operating museum, having opened its doors in 1824. Located in the heart of downtown, Pilgrim Hall is a treasure trove of 17th-century artifacts and Pilgrim possessions, some of which arrived on the *Mayflower*. You'll discover armaments like Myles Standish's and John Carver's swords, 1620-era pistols and armor, furniture and household items, period clothing, children's cradles, books, and art. Pilgrim Hall's mission is also to accurately depict the lives of the Wampanoag people (who existed for 13,000 years before the Pilgrims' arrival), as well as their complex relationship with the colonists. The museum has both permanent and rotating exhibits that reflect current thinking and encourage return visits. Pilgrim Hall also offers extensive online exhibits focusing on 17th-century architecture, colonial medicine, ancient navigational tools, and death and mourning, to name a few. And don't miss their *History in Progress* educational videos provided by local historians.

75 Court St., 508-746-1620
pilgrimhall.org

TIP

Pilgrim Hall is open Wednesday through Sunday, 9:30 a.m.–5 p.m., April through December. Don't leave without stopping in the gift shop for books, magnets, mugs, jewelry, Native American art, document recreations, prints, or other historic collectibles.

83

TAKE IN THE VIEW
FROM COLE'S HILL

With *Mayflower II* and Plymouth Rock getting all the attention, many fail to appreciate the historical significance of Cole's Hill located across the street and up a flight of granite stairs. The Hill offers a panoramic view of Plymouth Harbor, but its beauty directly contrasts with the hardship of the Pilgrims' first winter, when the Hill served as the colonists' burial ground. Its original function was only discovered in 1735 after heavy rains washed bones from the Hill into the harbor. You'll marvel at a magnificent sarcophagus bearing the intrepid colonists' bones and the words carved into its stone honoring them. A statue of Ousamequin, a Massasoit (or leader) of the Wampanoag people who brokered alliances with the colonists and helped them avoid starvation, proudly stands guard upon the Hill. One of the most beautiful spots in Plymouth, Cole's Hill is also the site of National Day of Mourning.

Cole's Hill, Carver Street
seeplymouth.com/listing/coles-hill

GET THE FACTS
AT JENNEY INTERPRETIVE CENTER

Interested in a traditional telling of the Pilgrims' experience in Plimoth? Visit Jenney Interpretive Center. Offering a more conservative and often opposing voice to the current historical interpretations, The Jenney's Co-Founders and Directors, Leo Martin and wife, Nancy, seek to educate on the impact the Pilgrims had on the development of the United States as a Christian nation. Dressed in period clothing, Leo Martin personally leads tours throughout Plymouth: a 90-minute interpretive walking tour that includes Plymouth Rock, Cole's Hill, Leydon Street, and Town Square, as well as a 45-minute interpretive tour of the National Monument to the Forefathers. Martin is a Plymouth historian with a wealth of knowledge and has appeared on podcasts of conservative personalities like Glenn Beck. Martin also leads a National Day of Prayer at the Monument of the Forefathers to continue the spirit of the Pilgrims' covenant.

48 Summer St., 508-747-4544
thejenney.org

TIP

If walking tours aren't your cup of tea, Leo Martin has developed PowerPoint lectures, which he presents indoors during inclement weather. In addition, Jenney Interpretive Center, the former Jenney Museum, has curated an extensive Plymouth history to explore—without the need for comfy shoes!

85

MILL ABOUT
PLIMOTH GRIST MILL MUSEUM

The Plimoth Grist Mill is a reproduction of the original Jenney Grist Mill that operated from 1636 until it burned to the ground in 1837. Rebuilt in 1970, this fully functioning grist mill has been in operation ever since. The Mill is part of Plimoth Patuxet Museums and is a fun interactive experience for the kids—they even get to shout a little—and a fascinating process for adults to witness. Watching the Museum millers place a 2,500-pound runner stone over a bedstone to perform the pre-automation-era milling process and describe the theory behind the procedure is captivating. Downstairs you will witness the huge face gear-wheel and smaller lantern gear-wheel as they transmit the waterwheel's power to turn the runner stone to mill the grain. Museum goers can purchase the Mill's organic stone-milled grains in the Museum Shop or order them online.

6 Spring Ln., 508-746-1622
plimoth.org/plan-your-visit/explore-our-sites/plimoth-grist-mill

TIP

Milling day is typically on Saturday afternoon if you're planning your visit and want to see the entire process. The Plimoth Grist Mill obtains its grains from local farms, and everything they mill is sold to local and regional restaurants and grocery stores.

TRAVEL THROUGH TIME
ON LEYDON STREET

Take a historical stroll down Leydon Street, the oldest continually inhabited street in the United States. Extending from Water Street to Burial Hill, Leydon Street is where the Pilgrims built their houses in the winter of 1620–1621. Although none of the original 17th-century houses remain, both 18th- and 19th-century structures line the road's eastern end. What catches the eye are the dwellings' diminutive sizes and tiny lots. Was everyone really that small back then? On the west end, sits Town Square and three historic sites: Burial Hill to the west, a who's who of historical Plymothians; the 1749 Courthouse Museum to the south, displaying an 1828 fire engine, a hearse, and other notable artifacts; and the First Parish Church on the north, one of the oldest continuously running spiritual institutions in the country. Take your time on Town Square, there's more than enough history to fill your day.

Leydon St.

TIP

If you're interested in local hauntings, Leydon Street is featured on several Plymouth ghost tours. It is believed the spirit of a woman murdered in the 1990s haunts her building. Tenants report TVs sometimes unexpectedly flip to her favorite program.

MEET THE TALENTED ARTISANS

AT LOCAL ARTS AND CRAFTS SHOWS

Plymouth is a hotspot for culture and art, so mark your calendars to meet the region's most talented creatives. Plymouth Library's annual summer Arts & Crafts Festival is a two-day event attracting more than 3,000 visitors and 80 accomplished artisans to sell their work and provide live art demonstrations. Also in August, the Plymouth Chamber of Commerce sponsors the Plymouth Waterfront Festival, now in its 38th year of hosting more than 200 talented regional and local artisans. Both events host live music while you discover one-of-a-kind glasswork and jewelry; handmade apparel, quilts, and handbags; metal and sea glass art; paintings, prints, and photography; and pottery, ceramics, sculptures, and wood art. Plimoth Patuxet Museums also gets into the act with their Winter Fine Arts & Crafts Fair in December. You'll find handcrafted gifts and live art demonstrations from 60 gifted artisans in addition to live music, a beer garden, and hayrides and hot chocolate for the kids.

pplfdn.org/4th-annual-arts-crafts-festival-2023
plymouthwaterfrontfestival.com
plimoth.org/events/plimoth-patuxet-winter-fine-arts-and-crafts-fair

TIP

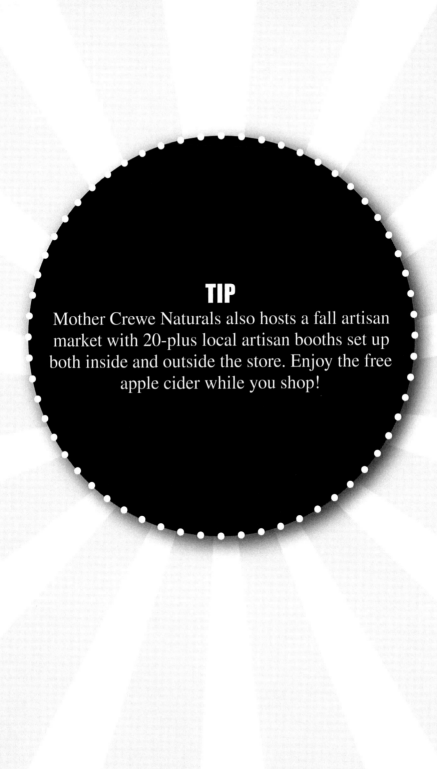

Mother Crewe Naturals also hosts a fall artisan market with 20-plus local artisan booths set up both inside and outside the store. Enjoy the free apple cider while you shop!

YANKEE

SHOPPING AND FASHION

MAKE IT OVER
TO MADE IT!

Made It! owners and local artists Sheryl Sousa and Joan Welch have curated a stunning collection of handmade gifts, cards, and fine art from over 150 local, regional, and national artists. Their goal is to make art accessible, and the variety and pricing of their gorgeous store items do just that. The blown and fused glass pieces are extraordinary, and there are plenty of ornaments, paintings and prints, games, puzzles and brain teasers, jewelry, metalwork, town-themed pillows, and pottery, priced for any budget. What catches the eye are the art tiles, beautiful and colorful renditions of beachy themes that are hard to resist—and why should you? Take one home. Check out their beautiful new location on Water Street, and if you're on the Cape, visit the other Made It! store in Provincetown. Both are the perfect places to find a unique gift for that difficult-to-shop-for person.

150 Water St.
301 Commercial St., Provincetown
508-591-0650
madeitplymouth.com

GET IT ALL
AT BRAMHALL'S COUNTRY STORE

It's hard to define Bramhall's Country Store. Is it a restaurant or grocery store? Ice cream shop or farm stand? Clothing store or florist? The answer: Yes! Entering the 1750s-era saltbox is like a trip back in time. And Bramhall's has been in the same family since 1828, so they must be doing something right. They're famous for their lobster rolls, Ben & Jerry's waffle cones, and corn on the cob, but there's so much more. Try their carrot tacos on hand-pressed tortillas, hamburger soup, or pumpkin ice cream pressed between two homemade Snickerdoodles. And don't miss the locally sourced fruits and vegetables at the farm stand. They also sell sweatshirts, tees, tanks, and even baby onesies. Oh yeah, they host live music and even sell homegrown flowers. Try the DIY flower buckets to create your own arrangement, or they'll be happy to make one for you.

2 Sandwich Rd., 508-746-1844
bramhallscountrystore.com

TIP

At one time the historic Bramhall's building housed one of the first post offices in the United States. The store is open from mid-May through December in the scenic Chiltonville village.

SUPPORT AN ARTIST
AT MOTHER CREWE NATURALS

Opened in 2023, Mother Crewe Naturals features unique artwork and gifts from throughout the region. It's a showcase for local artists run by local artists. Owner Alissa Hamblin says the shop is "based on Plymouth Folklore, and promotes local art, business, community, and history with every workshop, event, and purchase." To describe the clay gnomes, wood flowers, resin jewelry, pebble art, and stained glass would be impossible and wouldn't do them justice. Best advice: imagine 70 artisans channeling their creative energy into decorative gifts, artwork, crystals, paintings, clothing, candles, and soaps, and you'll get the idea. Discover art from Marsh Mud, Knotty Witches, Cove Way Crafts, Soulshine Naturals, Aroma Sparks, End to End Oddities, and many others. They host amazing workshops and events, like creative writing workshops, a DIY art bar, and a fall artisan market you won't want to miss.

11 Memorial Dr., 508-525-9736
facebook.com/mothercrewenaturals

HARVEST A GIFT
AT THE CRANBERRY HOUSE

The Cranberry House, perched at the harbor's edge, may be the perfect middle ground between the pretentious shouldn't-bring-your-kid-in-here gift shop and the touristy knick-knacky shops along the waterfront. You'll find caroler figurines, cards, keychains, books, magnets, scented soaps, jams, syrups, and an array of fun souvenirs to remind you of your Plymouth visit. You'll also find everything cranberry: dark chocolate-covered cranberries, cranberry sauce, cranberry mustard, cranberry tea, even cranberry taffy. The space is large and open, unlike many other downtown gift shops, and the sweatshirts, hoodies, and hats don't all have "Plymouth" emblazoned across the front. Don't bother with their website, it directs you to a Facebook page that hasn't been updated since 2019. If you're looking for something specific, just go in and ask or roam the aisles and get lost for a while. You are guaranteed to find something you'll want to take home.

145 Water St., 774-773-9871
facebook.com/profile.php?id=100063626947295

BRING YOU AND YOURS
TO LOCALLY YOURS

After six years in the business and one name change, Locally Yours is hitting its stride. Owners Alyssa Smith and mother, Pam, make a formidable team, specializing in Plymouth-themed apparel in their boutique gift shop. Their inventory isn't the standard fare you see in other Plymouth and Cape Cod gift shops, either. They design their own apparel and print the items locally. Their motto is "live your best life locally," and they're doing it—and sharing it. But the quality and designs also attract the discerning tourist who will find a touch of class and a distinguishing style that stands out in a cookie-cutter gift shop world. Enjoy their Plymouth Harbor map blankets, 02360 pillows, Brown's Bank sweatshirts—if you know, you know—as well as candles, glassware, New England–made jewelry, and an extensive collection of mind, body, and soul self-care products. And don't forget to swing by their Manomet location.

170 Water St., 508-591-7875
765 State Rd., 774-283-4056
shoplocallyyours.com

93

DUST SOMETHING OFF
AT SOMETHING FOR YOUR DUST

With what must be the greatest store name in Plymouth, Something for Your Dust offers unique and affordably priced gifts for the home. The goal, according to owner Dan Contrino, is to create a fun and interesting shopping experience for his customers, with items that they've either never seen anywhere else or that capture the imagination. Some items are vintage, like old cameras, typewriters, ancient trunks and steamers, maps, books, and antiques curated from auctions, estate sales, and clean outs. Other items arrive new from home-decor wholesalers and local artists, including small furniture, glassware, paintings, and ceramic art. The shop has an eclectic mix of classic and modern that will appeal to all. Customer Susan Ste. Marie said, "Something for Your Dust is just the best shop on Court Street. Dan [has] a wealth of knowledge about all things vintage and antique." Couldn't have said it any better myself, Susan!

16 Court St., 508-746-2203
somethingforyourdust.com/contact

TIP

The story goes that when one of Dan Contrino's family members would receive one of those nonessential holiday gifts, she would say, "Oh, something for my dust." You just never know what will inspire a store name!

94

FIND MORE
AT PLIMOTH GENERAL STORE

If you're looking for a little something—or a little bit of everything—Plimoth General Store is your place for one-stop shopping. This is an old-school, yet upscale, general store. Come on in for coffee or something to eat; they have great hot and cold sandwiches, soups and salads, and delicious bakery items. Don't miss donut Sunday, either. And while you're there, stock up on wines from Craft Beer Cellar, artisan cheeses, spices, oils, and items for your charcuterie board at home. How about a hat or some beachy apparel? They've got it. You can even shop here for kids' clothes and toys, jewelry, kitchen items, and home décor. Did I mention that they cater events and put together gift baskets? The building was once a bank and there's a little surprise for the kids in the former vault—sorry, no spoilers. Let them roam around back there and they won't want to leave.

44 Main St., 774-608-7933
plimothgeneralstore.com

TAKE A "TRIP"
TO LAUGHING MOON BOUTIQUE

If you haven't "Shopped the Moon" yet, get down to Plymouth and enter Laughing Moon Boutique's orbit. Owner Nancy Patterson once told *Wicked Local* her shop is a cross between "a Grateful Dead parking lot and a craft gallery." But even her description doesn't capture the "Sugaree"-sweet feeling you'll experience the moment you cross the doorstep. Amid the music and incense, Laughing Moon peddles signature repurposed and recreated clothing in vivid colors including tie-dyes, funky headgear, tees, skirts, and sarongs. You'll discover gemstone jewelry, dreamcatchers, pillows, wall art, keychains, and candles. And for a little spiritual healing, don't miss their stones and crystals, singing bowls, decks of tarot cards, and books. Patterson's hand-selected inventory creates a mystic "Om" vibe unmatched anywhere downtown over the past 30 years. There's something "shaking on Shakedown Street" . . . er, Court Street, that is. Pay them a visit, you'll be over the moon.

1 Court St., 508-746-0288
shopthemoon.com

FIND A GEM
AT THREE DAUGHTERS JEWELRY, APPAREL, AND GIFTS

Three Daughters has one of the best Plymouth waterfront locations with a stunning harbor view. But you won't even notice. Your attention will be distracted by the unique handcrafted gift items inside. This boutique shop features jewelry, clothing, and gifts selected from the works of both local and international artists. Their jewelry collection is expertly curated, and with names like LeStage, Cape Cod Jewelry, Dovera Designs, and Lola & Company, you won't find a better name brand quality and selection anywhere. Owner Joan Lyons has cultivated a relaxed vibe, where patrons can shop at their own pace in a no-pressure environment. Just as she told a *Boston Voyager* magazine reporter, Lyons wants her customers to have an alternative to online shopping, an experience where you can "shop by touching, smelling, and trying on what interests you." Join her for mimosas and refreshments during her special Sip & Shop events.

114 Water St., 508-747-3330
3daughtersjewelry.com

SPEND THE AFTERNOON
AT MAIN STREET MARKETPLACE

Don't call it a flea market! Give Main Street Marketplace its due respect; it's an antique mall with over 100 vendors peddling the most eclectic mix of nostalgia and collectibles you can imagine. The space is large and inviting, and it will take some time to browse all the different vendor spaces, especially when you discover the upper floor. You'll be transported into different eras as you discover books, records, decorative plates, nautical items, furniture, trinkets, jewelry, funky art, vintage clothing, knick-knacks, and just about everything else you never thought you would see again. Unearth that 1931 Rolls Royce car radio you had on your bedside table as a kid—you won't leave the store without it! Main Street Marketplace is a must-stop for rummaging in Plymouth, and a great way to enjoy a few hours downtown.

58 Main St., 508-747-8875
main-street-marketplace.business.site

TIP

The scuttlebutt has lingered that a few salt-of-the-earth employees may be a bit gruff. Sure, Plymouth folk can have a brusque demeanor at times—especially if the Sox or Patriots just lost a game—but you can't put a price on local flavor!

98

TAKE A PEEK
AT LOCAL MYSTIQUE

Local Mystique must be seen to be believed. This is a second-hand store like no other, with the most eclectic, funky, and out-of-this-world selection of strange, weird, and wonderful vintage items in Plymouth. Co-owners, Samantha Pike, and Joe and Kati Walsh are professional thrifters who made their passion a career. They hunt and dig for their antiques, collectibles, home décor, art, clothing, and jewelry not only with passion, but also with a vision. The store isn't as random as it may appear, and its appeal ranges to people of all ages. Their vinyl album and vintage clothing sections are a huge hit with the younger set, but the LPs and 45s lining the shelves—and the ceiling—will make even the older generation feel like kids again. Sam, Joe, and Kati all exude a powerful sustainability vibe, their store the perfect working example of successful repurposing in action.

398 Court St., 774-608-7485
localmystique.com

SHOP

THE ART SHOPPE JESSART STUDIO

Jessie Fries and Eddy Murray never expected to open a gallery, but these old friends knew they could work well together. So far, they've created a warm and welcoming venue for their stunning artwork at the Art Shoppe Jessart Studio. Each brings a different style to the table. Working as Coletta Craft Jewelry, Murray is a fourth-generation jewelry maker whose intricate, wearable art features pewter, silver, and copper often etched with vivid color accents. Fries embraces the canvas, and her charcoal and pastel drawings rival the intimate artistry of her acrylic paintings. Get on the schedule early because her popular art classes fill up fast! The gallery has relocated since 2014, starting in Plympton before moving to Carver, and finally settling into their downtown Plymouth location. Alissa Hamblin, owner of Mother Crewe Naturals, describes Fries and Murray as "generous and kind business owners and ultra-talented!" Visit during one of their art demos and watch them work.

84 Court St., 508-662-1432
facebook.com/theartshoppejessieeddy

100

PICK THROUGH THE PAST
AT FRESH PICK'D VINTAGE

Fresh Pick'd Vintage is another hidden gem, a vintage collectables store focusing on sustainability through repurposing. If you can think of it, Fresh Pick'd probably has it: handmade goods, coin wallets, handbags, eye pillows, beachy knick-knacks, books, dishes and plates, candles, furniture and home decor, antiques, soaps, arts and crafts items, and clothing. Owner Katie Denson provides great service with a personal touch, and she'll help match you with whatever you're looking for. They also have an awesome record room with over 500 albums—their outdoor record sales events somehow making the vinyl even more enticing! They are known to buy vintage items as well. Fresh Pick'd provides artsy workshops on metal embossing, customizing glasses or mugs, beading bracelet stacks, creating resin seascapes and treescapes, needle felting, and more. You'll also find limited-time pop-up shops appearing every once in a while to keep things fresh. Fresh Pick'd is a must visit in Manomet!

772 State Rd., 508-294-5762
freshpickd.net

ACTIVITIES BY SEASON

SPRING

SUMMER

FALL

WINTER

SUGGESTED
ITINERARIES

HISTORY LOVERS

BANG FOR YOUR BUCK

ART LOVERS

FAMILY FUN

DATE NIGHT

PARTY TIME

MUSIC LOVERS

OUTDOOR ADVENTURE

INDEX